The Singing Traveler

Songs from the Heart

Psalms 119

"As long as we have voices, we must sing."[1]
Laila Gifty Akita

I would like to thank the Lord Jesus Christ for giving me guidance when I write. I would like to thank my daughter Katelyn for suggesting that I write a book on Psalms 119. I would like to thank all of my family and friends who have encouraged me to keep writing.

Table of Contents

Foreword

Introduction

Song #1-"Please Don't Leave Me"   16

Song #2-"All of Me"   25

Song #3-"Open My Eyes"   40

Song #4-"Show Me the Way"   53

Song #5-"Turn Away"   67

Song #6-"Oh, How I Love Them"   81

Song #7-"Keep On Singing"   98

Song #8-"From the Bottom of My Heart"   117

Song #9-"For the Best"   138

Song #10-"The Tune I Dance To"   155

Song#11-"Smoke in My Eyes"   173

Song #12-"You Are Faithful"   189

Song #13-"Sweeter Than Honey"   216

Song #14-"Light My Way"   235

Song #15-"Oh I Stand in Awe of You"   248

Song #16-"Enough is Enough"   264

Song #17-"The River of Tears"   276

Song #18-"Consumed by Passion"   304

Song #19-"Sleepless Tonight"   323

Song #20-"It All Adds Up"   343

Song #21-"Nothing Can Make Me Stumble" 359

Song #22-"Singing Our Way to Victory"   380

Conclusion

"A bird doesn't sing because it has an answer, it
sings because it has a song." [2]
Maya Angelou

FOREWORD

I walked into the room and noticed the tables were set up and the decorations were breathtaking. We were there to hear the songs of the students who had worked so hard and tonight the recital would show us what they had learned. So as we were seated at the banquet tables and dinner had been served, one by one the students from the youngest to the oldest began to sing.

Some were nervous, some were not, some were singing the right tune, and some were, well, not so much. By the end of the night, though, it didn't really matter who was on key, and who was not. What mattered is that they all were doing what they loved to do.

Singing, most of us love to sing, some may sing in the shower, some may sing in the car, others will sing while riding their bike or while running in a race. Some singers are really good, and others may not be so good. Whatever the case might be, many of us like to sing. Music is a great inspiration, an outlet for some, and appreciated by a few.

I have been involved in music since an early age. My father liked to sing and play the guitar, so at the young age of nine, I decided that I wanted to play the piano. Lessons were not what I had expected, and wanted to quit many times. Through the years, I stuck with it, and now I have been playing for many years. One of the hardest things for me for a long time was what they call "transposing", taking a song written in one key and learning to play it in another key. In today's world transposing has become simple for those who might own an electric keyboard of some sort because you can push a button and transpose any song up or down.

In Psalms 119:54 the psalmist writes these words:
"I set your instructions to music
   and sing them as I walk this pilgrim way
(MSG).

 When I read those words, I knew that the psalmist liked to sing, and he would sing the Word of God as he traveled. Many hold to the belief that the psalmist here is David, because of the inspiring words and the exquisite form in which it is written. Others hold to the belief that in might have been Ezra, who would have written such words during the Babylonian exile.

There were many Psalms written by King David and we also know that David was a musician and so, therefore, let's look at some possibilities of why the author of Psalms 119 could be King David.

First, the structure of the Psalm follows the alphabetical acrostic, based on the 22 letters of the Hebrew alphabet, starting with Aleph and ending with Tau. There are 8 verses per alphabet letter which mean that each line in each section begins with the Hebrew letter. This is much easier understood in the Hebrew. This style of writing was a familiar style that David used in other Psalms as well.

Second, throughout the book of Psalms, only David referred to himself as "Your Servant" when talking to God.

Third, the phrase "turn to me and show me favor" is found in this Psalm and other psalms in which David was the writer.

Fourth, there were people in power such as noblemen, princess's and princes who sat around and talked about the psalmist, so we see that the psalmist was not a common man but a king, in which would point to David.

Fifth, the themes of Psalms 119 have a striking resemblance to Psalms 18, 19, 25, and 86 which were also psalms of King David.

Lastly, we know that David played the Lyre when he was in the court of King Saul. We also know that David sang to the Lord when he was delivered from his enemies.

When you put all these thoughts together it would suggest that David would be the writer of Psalms 119.

Let's stop and pause for a moment and think of our lives like a sheet of music. Most all music that has been written down, especially most hymns in the hymn book are written with a melody line which is the top line, and then three other lines which would consist of the harmony.

This is typically called the "score" which is a collection of different notes, which are put in different key's, tempo's and style's, much like chapters in a book or chapters of our lives.

Sometimes our lives are like the songs on a page our lives are in a major key, it is upbeat, snappy, and peppy. Then there are times when our lives are more of a minor key where they are slow and sad and maybe even frustrating.

All the writers in the book of Psalms felt the joy and happy days as well as the sad and lonely days. They expressed those feeling many times as they penned the words we read so often. The main theme that permeates throughout Psalms 119 is God's faithfulness and His presence. The Psalmist many times finds himself alone, persecuted and discouraged. He continually prays to God and meditates on the Word of God which is unerring, dependable, wise, reviving and corrective. The Word is a lamp to light the way of the Psalmist, and it has become the source of his delight.

We are all travelers on a journey we are foreigners in a land that we are temporarily living in. As we travel we should want to be like the Psalmist and become "The Singing Traveler", whether you are a great singer or a singer that could use some music lessons, be a singer. How does this happen? It happens when we respond such as the Psalmist responded by praying, by meditating on God's Word, and loving God more than anything in this world.

As you read through the pages of this book, it is my desire and passion that you will develop a love for God's Word and that you will meditate on it, memorize it, delight in it, obey it, and practice it. As you read through the pages of this book and through the pages of God's Word may we all allow His Word to shape us, and to be the guide for all of our thinking, speaking and our actions.

Psalm 119 is the longest chapter in the Bible consisting of 176 verses. There are only three verses in this passage that doesn't mention anything about scripture and they are verses 84, 121, and 122. The Psalmist calls God's Word **law, testimony, precepts, statutes, commandments, judgments, word, sayings, and ordinances.**

My desire is that you will enjoy this book, have a deep, deep love for God and His Word, study His Word and live it out, and dig deeper into the Word of God to pull out all the golden nuggets that are there for us to find.

Remember to sing as you travel through life, and let those songs come from the heart as you seek to serve Him and rely on His Word for guidance and a let it become the light that shines on your pathway.

INTRODUCTION

As mentioned in the foreword section of this book Psalm 119 consists of the 22 letters in the Hebrew alphabet. Each section is divided according to the letter. For example, 119:1-8 is the aleph section and each line begins with aleph. This is more recognizable in the Hebrew language than it is in the translated versions of the Word. There are 22 sections corresponding to the 22 letters (sin and shin count as the same letter, so 22 sections, not 23) of the Hebrew alphabet. This alphabetizing aids in memory. Once again it is an alphabetic acrostic. An acrostic is a poem or writing in which the first letter, syllable or word of each line, paragraph or other recurring feature in the text spells out a word or a message.

The Hebrew alphabet is not a collection of abstract linguistic elements, like the English alphabet. All letters in the Hebrew alphabet have names and identities. The Hebrew alphabet is among the oldest in the world, and it was either derived from or equal to the original Phoenician alphabet (even the word alphabet comes from the first two Hebrew letters: aleph and beth). In his book "In the Beginning: A Short History of the Hebrew Language", the author Joel Hoffman PH. D states, "....most of the reading and writing that goes on in the world today can be traced back to the Hebrews' experiments with vowels."

Within each chapter or song we will introduce the Hebrew letter associated with the eight verses, and explore into that particular letter and see how it fits into the section of verses it belongs to.

The following quote is from Michael Ben Zehabe an author, speaker and syndicated columnist whose specialty is the Hebrew language.

"Not only does every Hebrew word have its own definition, but every Hebrew letter, within the word, has its own meaning. God placed before you a great banquet of universal truths. All this in 22 Hebrew letters. Every letter contains a progressive curriculum designed to teach you about this marvelous world that God gave us. These letters will flavor each word's definition claiming its place in God's well-organized universe." [3]

Song #1

"Please Don't Leave Me"

"Don't leave, don't leave me here, I can't breathe without you." [4]
Author Unkown

Psalms 119:1-8

"Blessed are the undefiled in the way, who walk in the law of the LORD.

[2] Blessed are they that keep his testimonies, and that seek him with the whole heart.

[3] They also do no iniquity: they walk in his ways.

[4] Thou hast commanded us to keep thy precepts diligently.

[5] O that my ways were directed to keep thy statutes!

[6] Then shall I not be ashamed, when I have respect unto all thy commandments.

[7] I will praise thee with uprightness of heart when I shall have learned thy righteous judgments.

⁸ I will keep thy statutes: O forsake me not utterly." (KJV)

The above quote is probably the way we should feel about God. The Psalmist sums up the first eight verses by asking God not to leave him or forsake him. The picture I get from the words that he spoke is the picture I get from the above quote, knowing that if God left us, we could not even breathe because God is our life.

The first section of Psalms 119 starts with the first letter of the Hebrew alphabet which is **ALEPH**. The root *'alap* means to learn or teach. The identical word *'alep* means to produce thousands. The blessed or spiritually satisfied person is one who learns God's Word and teaches others as well.

The Psalmist who had seen much persecution and affliction throughout his life starts this song by reminding us that we are "blessed" if we walk in the word of God, and seek Him with our whole heart. He stresses in each of these verses how important it is to keep the Word of God as our guide

In my first book, I mentioned that God's way for us is a straight road, not a winding, twisting road. The Psalmist gives us the same idea here by telling us that we will be blessed if we "walk in His ways."

If you have read my first two books then you will know that I like to make things practical and analytical because I believe it makes it easier for us to understand. So I am going to try to break it down by verse, and then give us a conclusion to each section and relating it to our everyday lives.

Vs. 1-You are BLESSED when you
        STAY on course and are
        STEADY on the road.

Vs. 2-You are BLESSED when you
        FOLLOW His Word and direction and
        FIND Him with all of your heart.

Vs. 3-You don't
        WANDER off on your own but
        WALK in His way.

Vs. 4-God gave us the prescription for
        LIFE and He expects us to
        LIVE it His way.

Vs. 5-I should always obey so my
　　　STEPS will be
　　　STEADY and I will
　　　STAY on the course.

Vs. 6-I will not be put to shame if I
　　　CONSIDER all of your
　　　COMMANDS.

Vs. 7-I continually praise God as I
　　　SPEAK
　　　STRAIGHT from the heart.

Vs. 8-Please
　　　DON'T leave me because I am going to
　　　DO what you want me to
　　　DO!!

Blessed

When you read the first two verses of Psalms 119 we notice the word "blessed". Many times preachers and teachers like to tell us that the word "blessed" is translated as "happy". I think that when we insert the word happy in place of blessed it gives us and the reader the wrong idea. The word happy indicates a mood or a feeling in

19

our language in today's society. Let's take a look at the second verse on the previous page and we will replace the word blessed with happy. "You are happy when you follow His Word and direction and follow Him with all of your heart."

I'm not sure about you, but I know that many times in life I can be unhappy. I can still be following God, but find myself unhappy in some circumstances that I didn't expect to appear into my life. God doesn't promise us "happy". I think the better translation for the word blessed would be a fulfilling, and satisfying life when you stay on course and follow God with all of your heart. I just don't believe the word "happy" goes far enough in communicating the intent of the text.

Staying on Course

As a runner, I have found it satisfying and fulfilling to finish a race or a course. Many times I have run in the extreme heat or the extreme cold, and by the end, I haven't felt happy even though I have stayed on course and finished. The idea I get from these verses is that we must stay on course, not wander off to do our own thing, be steady and do what God wants us to do. In the New Testament,

Paul conveys the same idea to us by telling us in Timothy he has "finished his course". He also relates the same sentiment in Corinthians when he tells us to "run so that we will obtain the prize".

In 1993, a men's NCAA Cross-Country run was taking place in Riverside, California. There were only 5 runners who actually ran the 10,000-meter course while 123 runners ran only about 9,000 meters. Why? 123 runners took a wrong turn in the race shaving off some of the distance and escaping one of the steepest parts of the course. When Mike Delvaco decided not to follow the crowd and went the correct way, he was only able to convince 4 others to go with him. The 5 runners who stayed on course actually took the last 5 spots in the standings. Mike Delvaco could have protested because 123 men should have been disqualified. 5 runners stayed on course, and they finished knowing that they ran correctly.

Please Don't Leave Me

At the end of the eight verses, I found it interesting that the Psalmist would make this statement. "I am going to do what you want me to do but please don't leave me." I believe that this was more of recognition of the writer's weakness, knowing that he could not follow God on his own. He didn't believe that God would forsake Him, but he was making a statement that he would do whatever God wanted him to do, but he needed God to be with him when he sought out to do those things.

How about you and me? How many times do we try to do it all on our own? Many times I think that we have a tendency to do what God says to do, but then we leave God because we think we can do it without his help. Sometimes we do what God wants, but we rush God because we think that He isn't working fast enough.

Benefits

Take time to go back and read the first eight verses and notice the benefits that we receive if we stay on course and keep His Word. We are:

Satisfied

Fulfilled

No regrets

Full of praise

A right heart

SONG FROM THE HEART

Verse 2 would be the song in these first eight verses because we are blessed, and satisfied when we seek God with our whole heart.

So how do these things relate to our everyday life? I like the way Rich Young a United States Army Chaplain puts it.

"Obedience is seeking God with your whole heart. Performance is having a quiet time because you'll feel guilty if you don't.

Obedience is finding ways to let the Word of God dwell in you richly. Performance is quickly scanning a passage so you can check it off your Bible reading plan.

Obedience is inviting guests to your home for dinner. Performance is feeling anxiety about whether every detail of the meal will be perfect.

Obedience is following God's prompting to start a small group. Performance is a reluctance to let anyone else lead the group because they might not do it as well as you would.

Obedience is saying yes to whatever God asks of you. Performance is saying yes to whatever people ask of you.

Obedience is following the promptings of God's Spirit. Performance is following a list of man-made requirements.

Obedience springs from fear of God. Performance springs from fear of failure." 5

OUR PRAYER

Father, we thank You for Your Word. We ask for Your wisdom as we read and study Your Word. Help us to pursue and seek You with all of our hearts. Help us follow Your ways. We ask these things in Your name. Amen.

Song #2

"All of Me"

"Success in any endeavor requires single-minded attention to detail and total concentration." [6]
Willie Sutton

Psalms 119:9-16

[9] *Wherewithal shall a young man cleanse his way? By taking heed thereto according to thy word.*

[10] *With my whole heart have I sought thee: O let me not wander from thy commandments.*

[11] *Thy word have I hid in mine heart, that I might not sin against thee.*

[12] *Blessed art thou, O LORD: teach me thy statutes.*

[13] *With my lips have I declared all the judgments of thy mouth.*

[14] *I have rejoiced in the way of thy testimonies, as much as in all riches.*

[15] *I will meditate in thy precepts, and have respect unto thy ways.*

¹⁶ I will delight myself in thy statutes: I will not forget thy word." (KJV)

All of me, a single-minded pursuit of God is what stuck out in my mind when I read these verses. Once again the Psalmist points out that he is pursuing God with his whole heart.

The second letter in the Hebrew alphabet which covers these eight verses is the letter **BETH**. The word *bayit* means house in the sense of a building, but also means household; wife and children. This also serves to mean House of the Lord or Temple.

He starts this section with a question asking, "How does a young person live a clean life?" Then he answers his own question by "living out the Word". Then he once again states that he is pursuing God with his whole heart, with a single-minded attention and pursuit.

Vs.9-How do you live a
     CLEAN life? By
     CAREFULLY reading and living the Word.

Vs. 10-I am
SEEKING you with all of me and with a
SINGLE-MINDED pursuit so don't let me
STRAY and miss the
SIGNS along the road.

Vs. 11-I have
HIDDEN the Word in my
HEART so that I won't sin against God.

Vs. 12-Praise God, therefore, train me in the
WAYS of
WISE living.

Vs. 13-With my lips I will
reCOUNT all the
COUNCIL that
COMES from Your mouth.

Vs. 14-I will
REJOICE in your Word more than gathering
RICHES.

Vs. 15-I will
MEDITATE on every
MORSEL of your
WISDOM and I will attentively
WATCH your
WAYS.

Vs. 16-I will
DELIGHT in your Word and I won't
DISREGARD or neglect your Word.

IMPORTANCE

In the second section of this Psalm, we must ask
ourselves why it is so important to read, learn and
live by the Word. So how important is it?
According to the psalmist if we continually read
the Word, live the Word and learn the Word then
we will NOT sin against God. To me, this would be
the utmost importance of the question why. The
other important thing I gather from these verses
would relate to what I just said, but according to
verse 9, we also would be able to live a clean life.
Another reason of importance is we will be living
with more wisdom.

VALUE

How valuable is the Word of God to you? How
valuable is the Word of God to me? Are we like
the Psalmist in verse 14? What I am seeing in the
verse just mentioned is that we should rejoice so
much in the Word, that it would be like, or be

more than gathering wealth. Now, let's stop and think about that for just a moment.

Everyone likes to gather nice things everyone aspires to gather up some wealth so they can live in the world and not feel as if they are struggling. I want to ask it two different ways.

Do we rejoice by putting value in God's Word, just like we rejoice by putting value in our money or wealth?

You worked all day, it was a difficult day because your boss thought that he needed to yell and scream most of the day and sometimes you were the target of that anger. You can't wait until closing time, you are ready to go home and relax. Finally, the time has arrived; you clock out, get in the car and drive home. You get out of the car and as you are walking up the walkway to the front porch you decide to check the mail. You gather the mail and unlock the door you step inside your home and throw the mail on the counter you decide to sort through all of it. When you are tossing bills and unwanted literature out of the way you notice a piece of mail from someone you haven't heard from in a while. In haste you open the envelope and inside is a card that says "Just Thinking of You", as you open the card a check falls out and onto the floor. You skip reading the inside and pick up the check that has fallen and unfold it and start to rejoice because the check is for you in the amount of $200.

The unexpected check of $200 has you rejoicing, and you needed that check to help you through the week. Considering the kind of day you had it made that check even a greater reason to rejoice. You also know that the check is of some value. My point in the story above is to simply ask again the question, do you consider God's Word valuable like the check you received, and do you rejoice in God's Word like you would rejoice if some unexpected money showed up in your mailbox?

Do we rejoice by putting value in God's Word MORE than we rejoice by putting value in gathering wealth?

You graduated from college and you found a job that pays really well. You are now 22 years at the same job and have a few promotions that have increased your wealth. You have gathered all kinds of things with the money that you have made. You have a nice home, two nice cars that you use, and then a car in the garage that is a keepsake that you don't use very often. You have a boat, a house on the lake for vacations. Your bills are always paid and you take a vacation for a month every summer to a place somewhere in the world. This summer you have decided to go to Rome. You are prepared by buying the plane tickets and getting the rental car arranged and the hotel is paid for. You are excited. The day has come and your plane lands in Rome and you find your way to the hotel and you are rejoicing because you are off work and your vacation has started.

The first night you are relaxing in your hotel and you begin to think of all the things that you have acquired through the years of hard work and managing your wealth. You know there is a lot of value in all of the things you own, and you are rejoicing because you know that you have gained all these things because of your wealth. My point in the story above is to simply ask again the question, do you consider God's Word MORE

31

valuable than the wealth you have accumulated, and do you rejoice in God's Word MORE than the wealth you have gathered?

Look at verse 14 in two different versions and then ask yourself the two questions posed above.

"I rejoice in following your statutes
   as one rejoices in great riches" (Psalms 119:14 NIV).

"I delight far more in what you tell me about living
   than in gathering a pile of riches" (Psalms 119:14 MSG).

How much rejoicing do we do when we read, live and learn the Word of God? How much value do we put on reading, living or learning the Word of God?

"George W. Truett, a well-known pastor, was invited to dinner in the home of a very wealthy man in Texas. After the meal, the host led him to a place where they could get a good view of the surrounding area. Pointing to the oil wells punctuating the landscape, he boasted, "Twenty-five years ago I had nothing. Now, as far as you can see, it's all mine. Looking in the opposite direction at his sprawling fields of grain, he said, that's all mine. Turning east toward huge herds of cattle, he bragged, they're all mine! Then pointing

to the west and a beautiful forest, he exclaimed, that too is all mine! He paused, expecting Dr. Truett to compliment him on his great success. Truett, however, placing one hand on the man's shoulder and pointing heavenward with the other, simply said, How much do you have in that direction? The man hung his head and confessed, I never thought of that!"[7]

SONG FROM THE HEART

Verse 11 would be the song in this section of verses. We need to hide God's Word in our hearts, so that we do not sin against our Heavenly Father, God. There might be times when we do not have the Word of God with us, even though today we have apps for our phones and can have His Word on our phones. Now don't let that thought keep us from memorization. There are times when we are tempted to sin and when we are tempted we can't just pull out our phone or our Bibles and find a verse to combat whatever temptation is in front of us. We have to hide God's Word in our hearts.

In the book of Matthew, we are given a scene where Satan appears and begins shooting his fiery arrows of temptation at Jesus Christ. I am not going to put the scripture here, but it is found in Matthew 4:1-11.

Jesus Christ has just finished fasting for 40 days and nights and had gone out into the wilderness where He was met with the tempter, Satan. He was hungry after his fast and so Satan says to Jesus "Hey, I know you are hungry, but if you are really the Son of God, then tell these big stones to become bread." Jesus answered with scripture and said, "Man doesn't live by bread alone, but he lives by every word that comes from the mouth of God." Then Satan takes Jesus to the city and they go up on the highest point of the temple and Satan says "Alright, if you are the Son of God, and then throw yourself off, because the scripture says that your angels will catch you so that you don't fall upon the stones." Jesus answered again with scripture and said, "It is written down "Do not test the Lord your God." Then Satan took Jesus to the highest mountain and they looked out over all the kingdoms of the world and their beauty and Satan said, "I will give all of this to you if you will bow down and worship me". Jesus answered a third time with scripture and said,

"Get away from me, for it is written Worship the Lord God and serve Him only." Satan left!

Each time that Jesus was tempted He quoted scripture to Satan. During the second temptation, Satan used scripture as well, but he misquotes the scripture. The fiery arrows of Satan are always being hurled in our direction, we must fight back with the Word of God and there is no better way to do that except by memorizing the Word of God.

So where do we start? How do we begin to memorize the Word? You can find all the verses on love and memorize verses on different subjects. You can put the verses to music if memorization is a difficult thing for you. The Psalmist obviously put his to music as covered in the foreword of this book. In verse 54, he tells us that he puts God's instructions to music and sings them as he travels, and then they become songs from the heart.

One more thought on verse 11, I like the way the Message translation puts this verse down.

"I've banked your promises in the vault of my heart
   so I won't sin myself bankrupt" (Psalms 119:11 MSG).

I find this translation interesting because it conveys to me that if we deposit His Word into the bank of our hearts, then we won't have a tendency to go bankrupt by continued sin. What a fascinating thought.

I want to finish this chapter with the true and amazing story of Clyde Thompson and how the Word of God made a difference.

Clyde's father was a Bible salesman, but when Clyde was old enough to stay home alone, he refused to go to church with the rest of the family. Most Sundays, Clyde was out hunting while his family attended the church services.

In 1929, when Clyde was 17 years old he met some men in the woods and for some reason he killed those men. At the age of 17, Clyde Thompson became the youngest man in Texas history to serve on death row and to be sentenced to death in the electric chair. As the date of his execution neared, Clyde was listening to a radio preacher and asked for the preacher to come to the prison and baptize him. The preacher came and baptized Clyde.

There were some legal complications that arose and it kept him from being executed. So as Clyde was working hard at the prison work farm, things took a turn for the worse. He came up with a plan to escape and during the escape a number of other prisoners were killed in their attempt. Clyde was shot through the shoulder in one of his many attempts. While on death row he got into a fight and killed two other prisoners, now the number of people that were killed by Clyde became four.

As the years passed, Clyde Thompson was tagged by his own prison mates as the meanest man in the State of Texas. He developed such a terrible reputation inside death row that they put him in isolation. Clyde was transferred to another part of the prison, to an older building that used to be the morgue. A steel door was put in place and the only opening was about a foot square with bars. There was no running water and no electricity. The old building sat between two very tall buildings inside the prison, and he saw daylight for only six hours a day.

After being in isolation for two or three months, Clyde asked the guard to bring him a Bible. He knew they wouldn't give him anything else to read. He was bored and so he just wanted something to read. He decided he would try to prove the Bible wasn't from God because it was full of contradictions, well, that's what he had heard. So he began to read and the more he studied it, the more he became convinced it was God's truth. He came to realize that Christianity was man's only hope and he repented in tears on his knees day and night for months. Clyde kept reading the Bible and asking God if He could forgive a wretch like him.

Over the next few months, the guards began to notice the change that had occurred in Clyde Thompson. Later, he was released from the morgue and returned to death row. There, on death row, he taught and baptized by immersion eight other prisoners. He made such an impression on the prison administration that they finally release him from death row and let him go among the general population.

Clyde continued to study his Bible and he even took a two-year Bible course from a college in Tennessee. He became the chaplain's right-hand man. He even began sending articles that he had written to a Christian paper. After 28 years in prison, the State of Texas gave him a lifetime parole.

On the outside, Clyde went straight to the Lubbock County Jail, one of the largest county jails in Texas and he began a chaplaincy program there. Clyde Thompson died of a heart attack in 1979. It was Clyde Thompson who goes down in God's record book as one of the greatest soul winners. It was Clyde Thompson, the meanest man in the state of Texas, who literally led hundreds of men, women, boys and girls out of the streets of alcoholism, out of the streets of drugs, and led them to the foot of the cross of Jesus Christ. It was Clyde Thompson, the meanest man in the state of Texas, who was transformed when he allowed the Word of God and the love of God to take hold of his life. It was Clyde Thompson who rejoiced and valued God's Word more than anything else.

OUR PRAYER

Father, Help us to store up Your Word in our hearts and minds and allow it to guide our lives. Help us to find joy and value in the Word of God. In Jesus Name, Amen.

Song #3

"Open My Eyes"

"Open my eyes, that I may see glimpses of truth
Thou hast for me"[8]
Clara H. Scott

Psalms 119:17-24

[17] *Deal bountifully with thy servant, that I may live, and keep thy word.*

[18] *Open thou mine eyes, that I may behold wondrous things out of thy law.*

[19] *I am a stranger in the earth: hide not thy commandments from me.*

[20] *My soul breaketh for the longing that it hath unto thy judgments at all times.*

[21] *Thou hast rebuked the proud that are cursed, which do err from thy commandments.*

[22] *Remove from me reproach and contempt; for I have kept thy testimonies.*

[23] *Princes also did sit and speak against me: but thy servant did meditate in thy statutes.*

[24] *Thy testimonies also are my delight and my counselors.*"

As we enter into the third section of Psalms 119 we notice that a lot of the verses here would give great credibility that King David would have been the author of this psalm. Verse 17 starts with a prayer and its similar language is seen in many other psalms in which David was the author. Verse 23 talks about rulers and princes who seek to slander the Psalmist with their words; this would also point to King David as being the author.

The psalmist starts his prayer with a request in verse 17, and then in verse 18 he continues by requesting to God that his eyes would be made open so that he would be able to see all the wonderful things from the Word of God. The quote at the beginning of this chapter is from a hymn written by Clara H. Scott. Clara Scott had written many hymns and one day while reading Psalms 119:18, she penned the words to her most famous hymn "Open My Eyes." Two years later she was thrown from a horse and buggy and she was killed.

The third letter in the Hebrew alphabet is **GIMEL.** The verb *gamal* means to deal, or recompense in the sense of benefitting from. This is conveyed to

41

us from the beginning of the section when the Psalmist prays that God would "deal bountifully" with him.

Vs. 17-Be
> GOOD to your servant, be
> GENEROUS with me in life, I will
> OBEY your word and I will keep my eyes
> ON the road.

Vs. 18-Open
> MY eyes, so I can see and show
> ME the wonderful things from your Word.

Vs. 19-I am a stranger
> HERE in this WORLD, don't
> HIDE your WORDS from me.

Vs. 20-My
> SOUL is hungry, I am
> STARVING for your nourishing word.

Vs.21-You will rebuke the
> ARROGANT they are
> ACCURSED because they ignore you.

Vs. 22-Don't let those people
   MOCK me or
   MAKE a fool of me, I do as you ask.

Vs. 23-Though rulers
   SIT together and
   SLANDER me, Your
   SERVANT will meditate on your word.

Vs. 24-I find delight and
   CONTENTMENT in your words, they are my
   COUNSELORS.

DEAL BOUNTIFULLY

When you look at the literal translation of the beginning of the psalmist's prayer, verse 17 actually would read "Confer benefits on your servant". So my question when reading these verses would lead me to this. Do you think it is right to pray that God "deal bountifully" with us or to ask God for "benefits"?

Before we or I answer the question that was just given maybe we should give attention to the idea that God will deal bountifully with us if we are obeying His Word. Look in verse 21 in comparison to verse 17. The psalmist in his prayer asks God to deal bountifully in one verse and then speaks of God rebuking those who walk away or ignore God's Word.

In the New Testament in the book of Luke, chapter 6 we are told of how important obedience to God and His Word really is. Jesus Christ says, "Why do you call me Lord, but you don't do what I say?" Then he gives an illustration to prove his point. He tells the people in attendance that if you hear the words and you do those words then you are like the guy who goes down to build a house, he digs deep, lays a solid foundation on the rock. Then when the fierce winds blow and the rain comes down heavy, so that it floods, the house stays there and can't be knocked down, because it has been well built. He also tells those in attendance if you hear the words and you don't do those words then you are like the guy that goes down to build a house, but he doesn't put it on a good foundation. Then when the fierce winds blow and the rain comes down heavy, so that it floods, that house crumbles to the ground. The he finishes by saying that the house that crumbles is a total loss.

With the story from Luke and the psalmist's prayer, I would gather that the prayer for "benefits" is a prayer that has a condition. If I follow and do what God says then I receive the benefits that God bestows upon me. But if I, like the ones in verse 21, ignore those words, then I must face rebuke and chastisement for I have not followed what I have heard.

In answering the question above, I would answer it with these possibilities. First, this should be our prayer that God would deal bountifully with us because we will deal with us according to His Word. Second, this should be our prayer that God would deal with us so that I would stay free from sin and the worldly desires. Third, this should be our prayer that God would deal with us to bring us to a point of living a clean and pure life.

OPEN MY EYES

In the very next verse, we see our song title "open my eyes." There are times in our prayers where we must pray those three words, in order to see more clearly those things that we read in the Word, in order to see more clearly those commandments that God would have us follow, and in order to see more clearly our steps, and our lives and to know exactly where we are at.

When Clara H. Scott wrote the words of her hymn that we mentioned a few pages back, she mentioned four things.

Open my eyes that I may see glimpses of truth Thou hast for me.

Open my ears that I may hear voices of truth Thou sendest clear.

Open my mouth and let me bear tidings of mercy everywhere.

Open my mind that I may read more of Thy love in word or deed.

THE TRAVELER

In verse 19, the psalmist recognizes himself as a sojourner, a traveler that is just passing through this world. As a Christian, this is exactly what we are. There is an old song that gives such sentiments when it says "this world is not my home I'm just a passin' through". In 1 Peter we are commanded to not pursue the world because we are strangers and we are temporary residents.

46

The psalmist knows that he is just traveling so he wants clear direction from God. Then in the next verse, he needs that direction because he is starving and hungry for God's Word.

In the last chapter, we looked at the concept of whether we valued or rejoiced in the Word. In this chapter, we must ask ourselves if we are starving for the Word. Are we hungry for God's Word? Do we seek to learn it and read it as we seek food for our physical bodies?

One of the things that I notice in today's world, especially here in America is that a lot of us really do not understand what it is like to be hungry. We have, for the most part, 3 meals a day, we can snack when we want and stop at any convenience store to pick up something to eat or drink. I know for a fact because I go the convenient store every morning to get a donut and a drink.

HUNGRY

First let's define the word "hungry." It is the discomfort, weakness, or pain caused by a prolonged lack of food; To have a strong desire or craving.

Let's look at some things that might keep us from having a hunger for God's Word; these also would be the same things that would keep us from being hungry at meal time.

"Spoiled Appetite"

When you were a child or, at least, I know when I was younger, there were things my mom would not let me have in the afternoon because she told me that the cookie or candy I wanted would "spoil" my appetite. The very same thing happens in the spiritual as well. Many times we "spoil" our appetite by becoming full on something else like a TV show, a movie, we get full by playing a game on our smartphone or computer.

"One who is full loathes honey from the comb, but to the hungry even what is bitter tastes sweet" (Proverbs 27:7 NIV).

"Sickness"

There are many times when we become sick or ill that we simply do not want to eat. I know that when I have the flu or a bad sinus infection, food is the last thing on my mind. In the spiritual realm, this is also a cause why many do not want to feast on the Word, simply because we are sick. The cure for our sickness is to ask God to search our hearts, to examine us and to see why we are sick and not hungry.

"Search me, God, and know my heart;
   test me and know my anxious thoughts.
See if there is any offensive way in me,
   and lead me in the way everlasting" (Psalms 139:23-24 NIV).

"Swamped"

Sometimes in the life of today, we just become swamped, busy or simply distracted. Have you ever been so busy, so swamped with all you have to do, you don't eat, or you forget to eat? I worked at an oil company for many years, and sometimes we got so busy at lunch time, that I didn't have time to eat, or I would have to eat when I got a small break. Sometimes we don't think we have time for God's Word because we get swamped with things in life. We get busy with other things such as jobs, families, house projects, or church things that we have a tendency to neglect and we are too tired and not hungry for God's Word.

"Cast all your anxiety on him because he cares for you"(1 Peter 5:7 NIV).

 We need to make sure that we are hungry for God's Word by eliminating the snacks of other things. We need to make sure that we are hungry for God's Word by making sure that God the Great Physician gives us our physical and gives us a good heart examination. We need to make sure that we are hungry for God's Word by not overloading our plate with food that we won't eat, and getting rid of some of our business.

SONG FROM THE HEART

Verse 17 is the song in this section. As we have already seen and discussed this verse, we know that the psalmist prayer is that God would be generous, be good, or deal bountifully with him. More than those words, though, it comes down to the last part of the verse, "that I may live and do your Word."   In my book "Both Sides of the Coin" this concept is discussed a great deal, and so I won't go over it again here. James in the New Testament deals with it to a greater degree than we did here. God calls all of us to action. He wants us to be doers, not just hearers. I will narrow it down this way. Our attitudes will guide our actions. Our actions must be more powerful than what we hear, and say.

There is a story that is told of a pastor of a large church who had a dream one night that "opened his eyes". He dreamed that he could see his own church worship service on a particular Sunday morning. But there was something very strange happening in the service.

The choir was singing the mouths of the choir members were open, but no sound was heard. The people in the congregation were singing, but there was no sound from their mouths either. The preacher himself got up to preach his typical Sunday sermon. He opened his mouth to preach, but nothing, not a sound came out.

There was absolutely no sound at all in the entire worship center. Then, the pastor saw a little girl up in the balcony and heard her little voice singing, "Amazing grace, how sweet the sound, that saved a wretch like me."

The pastor was confused and suddenly woke up. "Lord, what was I dreaming? It doesn't make sense to me." The Lord spoke to his heart and said, "Pastor, you just saw a picture of what I see in your ministry and in your church every Sunday morning. People are singing and you are preaching, but I hear nothing. Your heart is not focused on me. You are focused on yourself. The only one I heard in your church last Sunday was the little girl in the balcony who matters to very few people in your church. But she matters to me because she came to church today with the right motive: to love me with all of her heart!"

OUR PRAYER

Father, Help us to have a hunger for the Word. Open our eyes, ears, hearts, and mouths so that we will see, hear, learn and speak of Your wondrous Word and Your everlasting love. In Jesus Name, Amen.

Song #4

"Show Me the Way"

"I do not pray for success I ask for faithfulness"**9**
Mother Teresa

Psalms 119:25-32

[25] *My soul cleaveth unto the dust: quicken thou me according to thy word.*

[26] *I have declared my ways, and thou heardest me: teach me thy statutes.*

[27] *Make me to understand the way of thy precepts: so shall I talk of thy wondrous works.*

[28] *My soul melteth for heaviness: strengthen thou me according unto thy word.*

[29] *Remove from me the way of lying: and grant me thy law graciously.*

[30] *I have chosen the way of truth: thy judgments have I laid before me.*

[31] *I have stuck unto thy testimonies: O LORD, put me not to shame.*

[32] *I will run the way of thy commandments, when thou shalt enlarge my heart.*

The word "way" or "ways" is mentioned in these eight verses 5 times. When we reach the last verse of this section the psalmist writes again about running. He speaks of running on the course that has been set for him. In one translation he ends the section of these verses by asking God to show him the way.

He obviously has faced a lot of hard times in life and is at the point where he feels that he can't go on by using words about "laying low in the dust", or at the point where he is dragging his feet, depressed. He has become sorrowful and he is lacking strength, but he knows that God's Word and his faithfulness to God will revive him.

The fourth letter in the alphabet is **DALETH**. The root word *dala* means to draw as in drawing water. The word *delet* specifically denotes a swinging door of a building. Since most doors open inward, this "thing you draw" is named after a going out of a house, or letting someone else in.

Vs. 25-I am
 LAYING down in the dirt, preserve my
 LIFE according to your Word.

Vs. 26-I gave an
 ACCOUNT of my ways and you
 ANSWERED me, so teach me your Word.

Vs. 27-Help me to understand the
 WAYS of your
 WORD so that I will meditate on your
 WONDERFUL deeds.

Vs. 28-My
 SOUL is tired and weary with
 SORROW, please
 STRENGTHEN me according to your Word.

Vs. 29-BLOCK the way of deceit
 BE gracious and teach me your Word.

Vs. 30-I have
 CHOSEN the way of faithfulness, at every
 CORNER I put my heart into your Word.

Vs. 31-I cling and
 GRASP tightly to your Word, so
 GOD don't let me be put to shame.

Vs. 32-I'll run the
      COURSE of your
      COMMANDS if you will show me the way.

DEPRESSION

The Psalmist was pouring his heart out. He had written in verse 25 that his "soul clung to the dust". He was spiritually dry, dragging his feet on the ground and he knew he needed to get back up on his feet and run again. Depression can be a terrible thing and sometimes we can become spiritually depressed which will lead to a physiological depression. Maybe you have felt like the psalmist and thought you were all alone in the world. Maybe you have felt like dropping out of the race of life and just have decided to sit on the side of the road. Spiritual depression is real, we deal with it at times, and the writer of Psalms 119 is feeling it as well.

The psalmist also overcame this depression and through these eight verses he teaches us how to overcome it as well. In order to overcome spiritual depression, it must be defeated. Here is the formula given throughout these verses.

1. Spiritual Quickening (vs. 25)

When you read verse 25 in the King James Version you will notice he uses the word quicken. Quicken means to arouse, stir or stimulate. He uses the word in front of the words "according to Thy Word". Essentially he is asking God in this prayer to be "stirred" or "stimulated" by the Word of God. Starting on the road to defeat spiritual depression the Word of God must be our guide and our plea in every prayer.

2. Stating Your Case (vs. 26)

The psalmist states, "I gave an account of my ways" sincerely and directly. We must, for our spiritual and mental well-being learn to tell God of our problems and our sins through the Lord. We must confess our sins to God and when we do this it will help us overcome them. Repentance comes from the heart, but our action is through our lips.

"This is the confidence we have in approaching God: that if we ask anything according to his will, he hears us. And if we know that he hears us—whatever we ask—we

know that we have what we asked of him" (1 John 5:14-15 NIV).

3. Seek God's Instructions (vs. 26-27)

He uses the words "teach me" and "make me". We learn the teachings of Jesus Christ through the Word, and we must be like the psalmist and be willing to be taught, no matter what the cost might be. We must also be willing to listen and learn from others who have gone down the same road. Our prayer, every time we read the Word, should be that we understand what God has for us. One of the best ways to overcome this spiritual depression is to learn His Word and walk intelligently in the ways of His Word.

4. Strength from God (vs. 28)

Any time in life that we want to be stronger in our physical bodies then we must exercise and lift weights. We also must be disciplined to use those weights. The same applies here if we want to be strong spiritually and defeat depression then we must ask God for strength as the psalmist has. His prayer is simply "strengthen me according to Thy Word". Our prayer must be the same. I read this statement the other day, **"to avoid the weight of** the world, one must work out with the weight of the Word."[10]

Remember the promise we have in the New Testament when we are told that "we can do all things through Christ, who STRENGTHENS us."

5. Separate Yourself from Evil (vs. 29)

Here is another verse that could possibly point to King David as being the author of this psalm. The Psalmists here prays "keep me from my deceitful ways". King David had this problem in the past. In 1 Samuel 21, David lied to Ahimelech and Achish, he would create a lie and then create another lie to cover it up. David obviously had a problem of deceit and he knew that he could fall into that pattern again, and so his prayer to God was to stay away from it. In our prayers, we must use this example and pray that we are kept from evil.

6. Set Your Heart on God (vs. 30)

The psalmist had chosen the way of truth and faithfulness. He follows up his thought on staying away from evil by choosing the way of truth and not deceit. The path to living a godly life and a life free of spiritual depression is to live in the truth.

To walk the path and the way of truth will result in true joy. We must use the truths in His Word to guide us on our walk.

7. Sticking with it (vs. 31)

The psalmist uses the words "I have stuck to Your Word". This leads me to an interesting thought because I find myself at times not "sticking" with it. Sometimes we will pick up our Bibles for a month or two or less and read it every day, then for a few months or maybe longer we only use it on Sunday. So are we sticking with His Word? But it would also convey the thought of "sticking to the Word" as not walking away from the truths that we learn from the Word. At the end of verse 31, he prays that he is not put to shame. This thought gives me the idea that the truths that he has learned, he wants to stick with them because if he walks away from them then he will be shamed.

8. Staying on course in obedience (vs. 32)

"I have run the way of Your Word" are the words the psalmist leaves here. Paul uses those same sentiments when he says "I have fought a good fight, I have finished my course". We must be willing to stay on the course, to obey God by running correct, running light by leaving weights on the corner, and running with perseverance and patience. When we do this, then the second part of verse 32 comes into play. God will show us the way; He will expand our hearts as we expand our minds to live by His truths.

The prescription to defeat spiritual depression is wrapped up in these eight verses. When we take the medicine that has been prescribed by living out these verses we will enjoy a healthy and fresh spiritual attitude. When we stray from the course that God has for us we suffer.

RUNNING

It has already been stated over and over in this section, but the psalmist really wants to stay on the right path or course.

I have been running for about five years off and on, probably more off than on, but during this time I have spent many hours running different courses, whether it is a race that I entered or just running through my neighborhood trying to find a different place to run. When I enter a 5k race and maybe it's a new one that I have not run before the course can be unfamiliar at times. In this case, I have to count on runners in front of me, because I am not usually, or never in first place. I try to look ahead when I am running so that I can see or notice any obstacles that might be in the way.

 One year I decided to put a race together, and I was also running in it as well. Since it was an out and back course, meaning that we ran on one side of the road out to a certain spot and turned around and ran back on the other side of the road, runners in the back would obviously see the runners up front on their way back. That day and most days I was about in the middle somewhere and as I was making a turn a bunch of people that were in the lead was headed towards me and they were yelling at me and calling things out to me that I am not allowed to put in this book. Since I had marked the course I knew it really well, plus I had run it before, I was not really for sure what the problem was until I returned back to the lobby of the building we were using. The problem was presented to me as soon as I returned because I guess there were some runners who had run approximately an extra half mile. The bike rider who was leading the group had missed a turn and led them down the road a little further than they were supposed to go.

The point I am trying to make is sometimes we can get off course, sometimes it's the "other" things in life than can get us off course. Sometimes in life, we can get so busy that there are many things pulling our hearts and minds in a lot of different directions and we can become sidetracked and get off course. Sometimes it can be other people who will get us off course. We must guard our hearts and minds and work hard at staying on course.

There are times in life when we become like the rabbit in Aesop's fable of the "Tortoise and the Hare". If you remember the story then you will remember that a rabbit challenged a turtle to a race. He did this knowing that he was a lot faster and so he figured he would show the turtle up by running fast and winning. What happened? The gun sounded and they both took off, well sort of, the rabbit shot out quickly, and the turtle moved slowly. If you are familiar with the story you already know the outcome, the turtle wins. How? The rabbit decided he was much faster so he had time to play around, take a nap, play baseball, and entertain others. The turtle, on the other hand, stayed at a steady pace. While the rabbit had played and rested the turtle was closing in on the finish line and by the time the rabbit had noticed, it was too late, the turtle had crossed the finish line.

We can take a lesson from the fable that Aesop presented. Like all runners, we must run with patience and keep a steady pace. Not veering to the right or to the left, but keeping our eye on the finish line.

Many times Christians operate like the rabbit. We run hard for a while for God, then we take a rest, or we play around. Then we run some more, then rest. Over and over the cycle goes and pretty soon we have lost our focus and gone off course. If we would live like the turtle, and by that I don't mean SLOW, I mean STEADY.

If you have ever run more than 3 miles then you know that you have to be steady, you have to keep a certain pace or you will tire out and most likely not finish or finish later than you wanted.

SONG FROM THE HEART

We have mentioned it already in this section, but the psalmist knew he had to stay on course and be faithful. Psalms 119:30 is the song here as the writer says, "I have chosen the way of faithfulness; I set your rules before me." Our course in life might be a short distance or a long distance according to our time. Whichever the case may be, we have to "stay the course" and run it faithfully.

"In the year 2000, there was a movie that came out starring Mel Gibson as Benjamin Martin, a reluctant Revolutionary War hero. This movie titled "The Patriot" brought in over $215 million.

In this movie Benjamin Martin has an 18-year-old son named Gabriel who is eager to join the conflict. Gabriel spent much of his time restoring an American flag. Tragically, Gabriel becomes a casualty of war and suffering deep loss, his father Benjamin appears ready to quit the fight. While Martin is grieving at the side of his dead son, the Colonel attempts to persuade Martin not to quit. He recognizes Martin has great influence with the soldiers and his leaving would demoralize the troops.

The Colonel says, "Stay the course, Martin. Stay the course." Grief-stricken, Martin responds, "I've run the course."

Resigned to the outcome, the colonel informs the troops and they ride on, leaving Martin behind. As Martin loads his son's personal effects on his horse, he finds the American flag Gabriel had successfully restored.

As the soldiers ride away, knowing for sure they had seen the last of Benjamin Martin, Martin appears in the distance, carrying the flag. With great determination, he rides upright in his saddle, facial expression for battle, and the flag waving in the wind. Martin has been a symbol of perseverance for the men, and there is a triumphant shout of both relief and excitement from the weary troops as they see "the patriot" crest the hill." [11]

OUR PRAYER

Heavenly Father, when we are spiritually depressed or defeated or spiritually dry, revive us according to your Word. Help us to stay on course, and to shun evil and not follow the path of sin. Show us the right way and we will follow with all of our hearts. In Jesus Name, Amen.

Song #5

"Turn Away"

"Repentance is a grace of God's Spirit whereby a sinner is inwardly humbled and visibly reformed."[12]
Thomas J. Watson

Psalms 119:33-40

[33] *"Teach me, O LORD, the way of thy statutes; and I shall keep it unto the end.*

[34] *Give me understanding, and I shall keep thy law; yea, I shall observe it with my whole heart.*

[35] *Make me to go in the path of thy commandments; for therein do I delight.*

[36] *Incline my heart unto thy testimonies, and not to covetousness.*

[37] *Turn away mine eyes from beholding vanity; and quicken thou me in thy way.*

[38] *Stablish thy word unto thy servant, who is devoted to thy fear.*

³⁹ Turn away my reproach which I fear: for thy judgments are good.

⁴⁰ Behold, I have longed after thy precepts: quicken me in thy righteousness."

The first thing I notice when I am reading these verses is the psalmist needs guidance, understanding, and direction. It seems whoever the writer is of this psalm, he was definitely a traveler, and in his travels, he wanted to make sure that he stayed on the right course. Once again he asked in the very first verse of this section, to stay on course and follow it until the end. I also see that he is of a repentant heart here, because he obviously had started living in a selfish way, wanting things that were just "things", trinkets, worthless.

The 5th letter of the alphabet is **HE**!! Some might believe that it is a prefix to the eighth letter *HETH*. The spelling and meaning of this letter or word are uncertain, but some might believe it stands for the word "lo" or "behold"! Others think that it is a prefix like a word "the" but is used less often than the way we use "the".

Vs. 33-Teach me
    LESSONS for
    LIVING so I can follow until the end.

Vs. 34-Give me
    INSIGHT, so
    I will keep Your Word and obey
    IT with all of my heart.

Vs. 35-DIRECT me with your Word for I
    DELIGHT in traveling this road.

Vs. 36-TURN my heart
    TOWARD your Word, not for selfish gain.

Vs. 37-Turn my eyes
    AWAY from worthless things, stir me up
    ACCORDING to your Word.

Vs. 38-FULFILL your promises to me, You will be
    FEARED.

Vs. 39-DEFLECT the harsh words I
    DREAD but Your Word is always
    DELIGHTFUL.

Vs. 40-Hungry for your
    PRECEPTS, through your righteousness
    PRESERVE me.

REPENTANCE

What do you do when you find yourself totally in the wrong? You repent! Repentance is recognizing when we are wrong, stop what we are doing wrong, and start doing what is right. In this section, the psalmist finds himself in this predicament. In verses 36-37, he prays that he will stay away from "selfish gain", and "worthless things". Before I go into the next few things I want to talk about, let's spend some time on repentance. Many times we are told to REPENT, but sometimes we are never told how or what steps are taken towards repentance. I have heard from many that if we just feel "sorry" for what we have done, then that is repentance. I have heard from many that if we just "confess" or tell, then that is repentance. What is true repentance?

First, there must be **RECOGNITION**. We must recognize when we have been in the wrong, when we have sinned when we have treated others wrong. So many people want to blame others for their wrong behavior. People do not want to admit they were in the wrong. Admitting to ourselves, to others and to God when we are

70

wrong will place us on the first step towards repentance.

Second, there must be **REMORSE**. We must have a genuine sorrow for the wrong we have done. Some would call this sorrow or remorse a "godly sorrow". The scriptures tell us in 2 Corinthians we should have "godly sorrow" and not "worldly sorrow".

"Yet now I am happy, not because you were made sorry, but because your sorrow led you to repentance. For you became sorrowful as God intended and so were not harmed in any way by us. Godly sorrow brings repentance that leads to salvation and leaves no regret, but worldly sorrow brings death" (2 Corinthians 7:9-10 NIV).

Godly sorrow is the hatred of sin. When we have godly sorrow it implies that we are willing to make a change with God's help. Worldly sorrow is not sorrow to make a change but afraid of being caught.

Third, there must be **RESIGN**. We must be willing to turn away from the sin, and forsaking the sin. We must be like the psalmist and not be willing to do the wrong again. It is a matter of making an

180-degree turn. Turn away from the wrong and turn to go in the opposite direction.

Fourth, there must be **RESOLVE**. Instead of looking back and dwelling on the wrong we have done or caused, we need to look forward to the things in store for us that will be better. We can never change the past, but we can change our future by taking care of the steps we take today. We must work hard and be resolved to make a change.

Fifth, there must be **RESTITUTION**. Whenever possible the person who has done wrong must make an attempt to leave the past behind and get on with their future. When we seek to make things right with the person we have wronged, then we clear our hearts and minds of guilt, and helps us to move on.

True repentance requires more than just saying "I'm sorry" or feeling "sorry". It involves these five steps and we must make an effort to move in that direction.

SELFISH GAIN AND WORTHLESS THINGS

The psalmist prayed that God would turn his heart towards the Word of God and not towards selfish gain. Then he prays that God would turn his eyes away from worthless things. How often do we find ourselves looking at things that are "worthless"? How many times do we become "selfish"?

I look at these words as one holding a bag. We are traveling on this road of life and we have this backpack or we have a suitcase or a big bag with us. Sometimes we find this backpack weighing too much and sometimes our bags are bulging at the seams. What are we putting in the bag?

Many times our bags are filled with long hours of hard work and no prayer. Many times we buy the latest computer, the largest TV, the best iPhone or iPad. Our credit cards are saturated to the brim with debts. We are bombarded on all sides and we have offers for exotic vacations, and we seek personal loans to purchase things we simply do not need. I am no exception!! In my household, we have a large TV, a few computers, and smartphones. We are tempted every day to keep our eyes on the things that we can't take with us when we die. Now, I will go on the other side and say some of these things we need in the world of today. I need a computer to write a book, I need a phone to make a call, and sometimes it's nice to relax in front of the TV.

Look at what the psalmist says in those verses. He didn't say these things were evil; he just wanted his eyes taken off of certain things. He didn't say getting nice things was an evil thing, but when they become selfish things then they are wrong. The time we spend on these things instead of spending time with God is what is wrong. Do you and I spend more time playing games on our phones, on social media sites, on streaming videos than we do with God? The psalmist prayer was to have less of the trinkets, and toys and have more of God's Word.

Many times we have a tsunami of temptations and we look at the worthless things and may lead us to sin and cause us to stumble spiritually. Satan knows our weaknesses better than we do and targets those areas. The psalmist was clear when he said "take my eyes away". Looking can lead to longing, longing leads to taking, and taking leads to a lifestyle that is unworthy of the child of God.

Keeping our eyes looking at worthless things becomes a waste of time. Time is a God-given commodity which cannot be replaced once it is gone. Simply stated, the time and resources we spend on worthless things are time and resources we no longer have available to grow. Looking at the other things will divert our eyes away from teaching, preaching, singing, and praising God.

So what does this all mean? Does this mean we can't have nice things? Does this mean we can't go out and shop for a new car, or buy a new TV? Does this mean we must sit and never do anything else, only pray, read our Bibles, and go to church? NO!! Look what Paul says in Philippians 4.

"Finally, brothers and sisters, whatever is true, whatever is noble, whatever is right, whatever is pure, whatever is lovely, whatever is admirable—if anything is excellent or praiseworthy—think about such things" (Philippians 4:8 NIV).

The verse above covers a lot of areas – from a beautiful painting to a heart-stirring musical composition, to a time-tested work of literature, to an honorably-waged athletic competition, to an expertly crafted piece of furniture. God has given us as humans with creative abilities, so we can promote what is true, what is beautiful and good. Our job is to make those things a priority and "take our eyes off" those things which have no lasting value.

SONG FROM THE HEART

We have already covered the song in this section throughout the last few paragraphs, but the verse is Psalms 119:37 "Divert my eyes from toys and trinkets, invigorate me on the pilgrim way." I like that translation because sometimes those worthless things are nothing but toys and trinkets. The traveler continues to sing, sometimes he is singing praises to God, and sometimes they are prayers to God.

People all around us are pursuing things that have no lasting value. A classical short story written by Anton Chekhov called, "The Bet" talks about such pursuits. This story will give us an insight to people and what they place value on.

The plot involves a wager between two educated men regarding solitary confinement. A wealthy, middle-aged banker believed the death penalty was a more humane penalty than solitary confinement because "an executioner kills at once, solitary confinement kills gradually." One of his guests at a party, a young lawyer of twenty-five, disagreed, saying, "To live under any conditions is better than not to live at all."

Angered, the banker impulsively responded with a bet of two million rubles that the younger man could not last five years in solitary confinement. The lawyer was so convinced of his endurance that he announced he would stay fifteen years alone instead of only five.

The arrangements were made, and the young man moved into a separate building on the grounds of the banker's large estate. He was allowed no visitors or newspapers. He could write letters but receive none. There were guards watching to make sure he never violated the agreement, but they were placed so that he could never see another human being from his windows. He received his food in silence through a small opening where he could not see those who served him. Everything else he wanted—books, certain foods, musical instruments, etc.—were granted by special written request.

During the first year, the piano could be heard at almost any hour, and he asked for many books, mostly novels and other light reading. The next year the music ceased and the works of various classical authors were requested. In the sixth year of his isolation, he began to study languages and soon had mastered six. After the tenth year of his confinement, the prisoner sat motionless at the table and read the New Testament. After more than a year's saturation of the Bible, he began to study the history of religion and works on theology.

The second half of the story focuses on the night before the noon deadline when the lawyer would win the bet. The banker was now at the end of his career. His risky speculations and impetuosity had gradually undermined his business. The once self-confident millionaire was now a second-rate banker, and it would destroy him to pay off the wager. Angry at his foolishness and jealous of the soon-to-be-wealthy lawyer who was now only forty, the old banker determined to kill his opponent and frame the guard with the murder. Slipping into the man's room, he found him asleep at the table and noticed a letter the lawyer had written to him. He picked it up and read the following:

Tomorrow at twelve o'clock I shall be free . . . but before leaving this room . . . I find it necessary to say a few words to you. With a clear conscience, and before God, who sees me, I declare to you that I despise freedom and life and health and all that your books call the joys of this world. . . . I know I am wiser than you all. . . . And I despise all your books; I despise all earthly blessings and wisdom. All is worthless and false, hollow and deceiving like the mirage. You may be proud, wise and beautiful, but death will wipe you away from the face of the earth, as it does the mice that live beneath your floor; and your heirs, your history, your immortal geniuses will freeze or burn with the destruction of the earth. You have gone mad and are not following the right path. You take falsehood for truth and deformity for beauty. To prove to you how I despise all that you value I renounce the two million on which I looked, at one time, as the opening of paradise for me, and which I now scorn. To deprive myself of the right to receive them, I will leave my prison five hours before the appointed time, and by so doing break the terms of our compact.

The banker read the lines, replaced the paper on the table, kissed the strange, sleeping man and with tears in his eyes, quietly left the house. Chekhov writes, "Never before, not even after sustaining serious losses on change, had he despised himself as he did at that moment." His tears kept him awake the rest of the night. And at seven the next morning he was informed by the watchmen that they had seen the man crawl through a window, go to the gate, and then disappear. 13

OUR PRAYER

Heavenly Father, we ask today that you would help us to learn more about repentance, and when we have wronged others, we pray that we would make it right. We also need help to focus on Your Word, and not on the selfish, worthless things that take our attention away from You. In Jesus Name, Amen.

Song #6

"Oh, How I Love Them"

"Within the covers of the Bible are the answers for all the problems men face."[14]
Ronald Reagan

Psalms 119:41-48

[41] *"Let thy mercies come also unto me, O LORD, even thy salvation, according to thy word.*

[42] *So shall I have wherewith to answer him that reproacheth me: for I trust in thy word.*

[43] *And take not the word of truth utterly out of my mouth; for I have hoped in thy judgments.*

[44] *So shall I keep thy law continually for ever and ever.*

[45] *And I will walk at liberty: for I seek thy precepts.*

[46] *I will speak of thy testimonies also before kings, and will not be ashamed.*

[47] *And I will delight myself in thy commandments, which I have loved.*

[48] My hands also will I lift up unto thy commandments, which I have loved; and I will meditate in thy statutes."

Ronald Reagan became the 40th president of the United States of America and occupied this prestigious position from 1981 to 1989. Reagan believed that America needed the Bible. He believed the Bible held all the answers. More than once he stated that he was accused of being simplistic. The quote at the beginning of this chapter was a line that many found over-the-top, some White House staff among them. Ronald Reagan believed it with great devotion. When he shared the above quote before the National Religious Broadcasters convention, they said it "brought the house down." The audience responded with a standing ovation and Reagan was delighted. In the 6th section of this psalm, the psalmist talks about having freedom because of the Word, and he believes in obeying it, speaking it, meditating on it, delighting in the Word, and loving the Word.

The 6th letter in the Hebrew alphabet is **WAW**! Sometimes these letters were named after the shape they looked like when written down. *Waw* means hook or a peg and is strictly reserved for the hook or pegs that kept the curtains of the tabernacle in place. Some believed that the shape reminds them of a peg.

Vs. 41-May your unfailing love
        SHAPE my life with
        SALVATION just as you promised.

Vs. 42-THEN I can answer anyone who
        TAUNTS me, because I
        TRUST your Word.

Vs. 43-Never
        DEPRIVE me of your Word, I
        DEPEND on your commandments.

Vs. 44-I will always
        OBEY your law,
        OH, I will guard it forever.

Vs. 45-I will
        LIVE in freedom and I will
        LOVE your truth.

Vs. 46-I will
SPEAK of your
STATUTES before kings, and will not be
SHAMED.

Vs. 47-DELIGHTED with your Word, oh I
DO love them.

Vs. 48-I
CHERISH your Word and I meditate on Your
COUNSEL.

FREEDOM OR RESTRICTIONS

What do you think about when you pick up the Word of God and start reading? Do you think it is a book of freedom or a book full of restrictions? I have spoken to people who think the Bible is nothing but a bunch of rules that we must follow and they don't want to be bound by such "restrictions".

In James 1 and in James 2, it talks about the "law of liberty", the word "law" meaning God's Word, and the word "liberty" meaning freedom. The writer of Psalms 119 states, "I will keep your law forever, and he follows up this thought with the words "I shall walk in a wide place". The statement in verse 45 also translates "I will walk in liberty". The writer is equating God's Word with freedom.

Some might think that living without the Word of God gives us freedom. In reality, the Word of God is freedom and disobedience, or going against God's Word becomes bondage. Disobedience ties our hearts up with guilt, regrets, consequences of our wrong choices, anxiety, and many other problems. When we live in obedience to God's Word, we have a freedom that living disobediently can't provide.

Not too long ago, I had been reading some "Warning Labels" on different products and some of these warnings were actually hilarious and made me wonder why they would have to actually put those on that product.

On the cord of a hair straightener, the label reads "this product can burn eyes". Now I don't use one of these but I know people that have and so far I have not come in contact with any of those people who thought they would try to straighten out their eyelashes with a straightener.

The inside label on a child's garment read "Wash inside out, remove child before washing." My children are grown now, but I can't remember a time when I tried to wash my children's clothing with them still inside.

On a package of fishing lures attached was this warning, "harmful is swallowed". Now I have done quite a bit of fishing and I wonder who this warning is aimed at, the fish or the fisherman? Maybe you go out to fish, and you have been out there so long, you get hungry and so you look at all those brightly colored lures and think "those look tasty." I really don't think you are going to try any of those out for a snack.

There is a carpenter's router which had this warning, "this product not intended for use as a dental drill." I am not sure if there were two guys sitting around in a garage one day, and one guy had a toothache and the other one decided he would fix it with a router.

There are warnings for us all through life, they are on products, there are road warnings, there are warning for floods, and tornados. It seems someone somewhere is always telling us what we can't do. Some people believe this is the essence of Christianity. They think God is sitting up in heaven on the throne handing out rules like lawyers, and commanding us "don't do this, and don't do that, and don't you dare have any fun!"

Christianity has become a drudgery for many instead of freedom. This is a real tragedy! God is all about freedom and through Him is where we experience real freedom.

Many times in our culture people believe that freedom is being set free for the shackles of religion. Many want to reject the teaching of scripture and choose their own beliefs. They consider themselves free.   Many people that I have come in contact with believe the Bible is restrictive. They believe if they choose to follow the Bible then they will not have the freedom to live as their friends do.

In the New Testament, in the book of John, Jesus is talking to a group of Pharisees and he is sharing with them the contrast of freedom and slavery.

31 To the Jews who had believed him, Jesus said, "If you hold to my teaching, you are really my disciples.32 Then you will know the truth, and the truth will set you free."

33 They answered him, "We are Abraham's descendants and have never been slaves of anyone. How can you say that we shall be set free?"

34 Jesus replied, "Very truly I tell you, everyone who sins is a slave to sin.35 Now a slave has no permanent place in the family, but a son belongs to it forever. 36 So if the Son sets you free, you will be free indeed. 37 I know that you are Abraham's descendants. Yet you are looking for a way to kill me, because you have no room for my word. 38 I am telling you what I have seen in the Father's presence, and you are doing what you have heard from your father" (John 8:31-38 NIV).

Usually, when we hear the word "slavery" it brings up bad connotations in our mind of the days of the "Civil War." In America in the years that we are living in, we find slavery to be repulsive and just outright wrong. When you stop and think of the word "slavery", you undoubtedly get a picture in your mind of what you think slavery entails.

Earlier I mentioned that when we live in disobedience to the Word of God then we become enslaved. By looking at the verses in John, what are we slaves of?

SIN

In verse 34 of John 8, Jesus says, "everyone who sins is a slave to sin." When we are disobedient to the commands and Word of God, then we have sinned, and that sin can become our Master. Maybe there are some certain sins that have become a master over you?

There are quite a few different sins mentioned in the New Testament and I don't have the time or space to go over all of them, but let's pull out a few and see if they would be ones that could be our Master.

Drinking Alcohol-Now I could get into this really deep but I won't. I just believe that alcohol is very addictive and it can actually become a master over you if you continue to use it on a regular basis. Some people believe they can stop at any time, or they use the excuse they only drink on occasion. When alcohol becomes the preferred drink at every outing, restaurant, or every meal, then I believe it is starting to be your master. There have been tests done and these tests show that after drinking three beers, you have an average memory loss of 13%. After drinking small quantities of alcohol some trained typists were tested and their errors increased by over 40%. One ounce of alcohol increases the time required to make a decision by 10%, it hinders muscular reaction by 17%, and lack of attention is increased by over 35%. Pastor Greg Laurie said this about Christians and alcohol.

"Among the sobering statistics about alcohol consumption in the U.S.: In 2010, 211 children were killed in drunk-driving crashes. Out of those 211 deaths, 131 (62 percent) were riding with the drunk driver. Also, adults who drank too much and got behind the wheel amounted to 112 million times, two years ago. That is almost 300,000 incidents of drinking and driving each day, according to the Center of Disease Control and Prevention.

Perhaps one of the most revealing statistics about the harm of alcohol abuse, three out of every four convicted jail inmates were involved in alcohol or drugs at the time of their current offense, according to statistics cited on the faith-based recovery website, MartyAngelo.com.

'I can't think of a single good thing that comes from drinking, but I can think of many bad things that come from it: broken homes, violence, accidents, people killed on the road by drunk drivers, addiction, destroying your health . . . the list goes on.'"[15]

Pornography-Many Christians, especially men, would never admit to looking at pornography because most would do it in private. Since there is such an easy access to porn today, it has made it easier for someone to use it on a regular basis. Pornography has become a $97 billion worldwide. Over 50% of pastors say that porn is a temptation, 40% say that it is a current struggle. Over 30% of Christians say it is alright to view pornography on a regular basis. Over 50% of all evangelical pastors say they have viewed porn.

Anger-This sin can become your Master really fast, I know, because I have dealt with this in my own life for a very long time. Do Christians battle this? I believe it is bigger than what people want to believe it is. Moses in the Old Testament had an anger problem, and that is one of the things that kept him from entering into the Promised Land. In the New Testament, we are told to get rid of anger. We are commanded over and over throughout God's Word to be "slow to anger." Most people who are behind bars are there because of an "anger issue."

There are many other sins that can become our masters such as complaining, bitterness, lust, lying, greed, and selfishness.

SPIRITUAL ARROGANCE

The Pharisees were the classic bunch that had this as their slave. The lesson given in the book of Luke shows how this was a problem for the Pharisees. The tax collector and the Pharisee had gone to the temple to pray. The tax collector stood over in the corner and prayed to God with his head bowed using these words, "Lord have mercy on me, I am a sinner." The Pharisee stood proudly in the middle of the temple and proclaimed these words, "God, I thank you that I am not like other men, robbers, evildoers, adulterous, or like this tax collector.

Do Christians today act like this? Yes, I believe there are some that do. I believe there are ones who walk around with their chest held high believing they are better than those around them. They may not pray the prayer the Pharisee prayed, but their arrogance is seen by many as they walk through the doors of their church. We must simply come to God, knowing we are sinners, and humbly worshiping as we pray.

SLIGHTING GOD

In the passage above Jesus says to the Pharisees, "you are trying to kill me, and you have no room for my word." We block God out of our lives when we don't follow His Word, or do His commands. How many times do we find ourselves not "having time" for His Word? We make excuses that we do not have time to read it, but we will spend hours on social media. We don't have time to read His Word, but we will read all kinds of other material. We might not be physically trying to kill Jesus, but are we killing Him with our lack of zeal? Are we killing Him when we refuse to pray to Him?

If you feel a distance between you and God, it is probably because of your disobedience in not following His Word or neglecting it all together.

So where is this freedom? Where do we get it?

First, we have to have obedience to God's Word. The psalmist writes, "I walk in freedom for I have sought out Your Word." When we submit to the Word of God it sets us free from a host of slaveries. The Word of God warns us of the destructive things that are trying to enslave us.

Second, there is great power in the Spirit-inspired Word of God. It releases you from slavery to sin, slavery to spiritual arrogance, and from our tendency to slight God.

Third, we have to willingly submit to the Word of God. If we want freedom, then we have to follow the teachings of Jesus and let those teachings from His Word sink deep into our hearts and minds.

Do you feel free today? If not, take the time right now to write down on a piece of paper the sin that you believe is enslaving you. It may be a sin like lust, bitterness, gossip, substance abuse, pornography, lying, greed, alcohol or depression. Maybe it is the sin of fear or anxiety or hatred. Name it!! Write it down!!!

Now that you have written down and named the sin or sins that enslave you, I want you to declare freedom over this in the name of Christ. Remember Jesus said these words, "Then you will know the truth, and the truth will set you free."

To finish this thought out, now take that piece of paper, pray about it, and proclaim out loud that you are free from this binding sin.

"It is for freedom that Christ has set us free. Stand firm, then, and do not let yourselves be burdened again by a yoke of slavery" (Galatians 5:1 NIV).

SONG FROM THE HEART

We have spent a lot of time on the song which are found in verses 44-45. The psalmist, in essence, says that "he will walk freely." This must be our goal and this must be our aim to be free from the power of sin. Let's finish up by remembering this:

WE are **FREE** from the **PENALTY** of sin because of Christ's work on the cross.

WE are **FREE** from the **POWER** of sin because of Christ's work in our lives.

WE will be **FREE** from the **PRESENCE** of sin when Christ's returns and takes us **HOME**.

As Christians, we can escape the slavery of sin. We are no longer headed on the "highway to hell" but because of Jesus death on the cross he bought us a ticket on the Freedom Train.

Do you remember the story of Harriet Tubman?

Born a slave on Maryland's eastern shore, she endured the harsh existence of a field hand, including brutal beatings. In 1849 she fled slavery, leaving her husband and family behind in order to escape. After her escape, she was able to get to the North with the help of some sympathetic people both white and black. She was so thankful for the help she received she decided to risk her own life to become a conductor on the Underground Railroad. Despite the bounty on her head, she returned to the South at least

19 times to lead her family and over 300 others to freedom.

OUR PRAYER

Heavenly Father, please take away the bondage of our past disobedience and set us free to worship and serve You with clean hearts and minds. We want to thank You for the freedom we have in following You and Your Word. In Jesus Name, Amen.

Song #7

"Keep On Singing"

"Only knowing one part to a song so you just keep singing the same line for the whole day." **16**
Unknown

Psalms 119:49-56

[49] *Remember the word unto thy servant, upon which thou hast caused me to hope.*

[50] *This is my comfort in my affliction: for thy word hath quickened me.*

[51] *The proud have had me greatly in derision: yet have I not declined from thy law.*

[52] *I remembered thy judgments of old, O LORD; and have comforted myself.*

[53] *Horror hath taken hold upon me because of the wicked that forsake thy law.*

[54] *Thy statutes have been my songs in the house of my pilgrimage.*

[55] *I have remembered thy name, OLORD, in the night, and have kept thy law.*

[56] *This I had, because I kept thy precepts.*

The psalmist in verse 54 talks about singing songs of God's Word. We have talked about this in the beginning of this book. I found this verse amazing maybe because I am a musician myself and have written songs and sang many songs. There have been many worship songs over the last number of years that have been written using the Word of God. I have listened to a lot of music and been around music for a long time, I believe that when we are reading the Word of God, especially songwriters, God will use that Word to inspire some great songs.

The psalmist obviously had taken the time to use the Word, and as he was traveling from house to house and town to town, he would sing the scriptures. He talks about the promises of God, the hope of God, and finding comfort, singing as he traveled, and meditating on God's Word deep into the night.

The 7th letter of the Hebrew alphabet is **ZAYIN**. This actually means debated. Some have the belief that a form of *zayin* represents a hand weapon. The identical root of the word which is *zwz* means abundance or fullness.

Vs. 49-Remember
>WHAT You said to me, I
HANG on to the
WORDS of
HOPE.

Vs. 50-My comfort in
>MY sufferings are Your
PROMISES for they
PRESERVE me.

Vs. 51-The arrogant
>RIDICULE me unmercifully, Your
REVELATION I do not stray from.

Vs 52-Your ancient
>LAWS I remember
LORD, they are my comfort.

Vs. 53-INDIGNATION grips me because they
>IGNORE your laws.

Vs. 54-I
>SET your Word to music, I
SING them as I travel.

Vs. 55-In the
>NIGHT I meditate on Your
NAME, I keep your Word.

Vs. 56-My normal
        PRACTICE is to keep Your
        PRECEPTS.

In the very first verse of this section, he talks about hope.

HOPE

In the last few years, I have officiated 3 funerals, and they were all family members of the same family. One thing that I would always try to stress in each sermon was the fact of "hope." The older I get and the longer I live and the things that I see, I often wonder how people make it through life when they don't have any sense of hope. The psalmist knew that his hope was in God.

I believe that we have all lost hope somewhere along our journey. Maybe you lost hope when you realized your sports team wasn't going to win the game. Maybe it was more serious than that, maybe you were at a point of losing your job or you had a serious health problem. Maybe a family member was at the brink of death.   Maybe you are depressed and you don't know what else to do or how to turn it around. Maybe your life seems to be spiraling out of control. Maybe you are on the edge of disaster, and you don't see any way for it to turn around. I've been in some of those scenarios; I've lived some of those "maybe's".

During those times, perhaps you want to take the advice of Job's wife and "curse God and die."

Right now, as I am typing and watching the words come up on the screen, I know of people who are battling with "hope".

Never give up hope, is what I would have to say today because for the Christian life is essentially a life of hope. As a child of God, you have hope. Hope is necessary to the human spirit as oxygen is to the physical body. A lack of hope can literally destroy your life. The lack of hope brings on the feelings of senselessness, purposelessness, and despair.

The word "hope" is mentioned more than 53 times in the New Testament. Paul mentions the word "hope" 35 times from the book of Romans to Titus, and he mentions it 6 times in the book of Hebrews.

One of the greatest verses that I have read about hope is found in Romans.

"May the God of hope fill you with all joy and peace as you trust in him, so that you may overflow with hope by the power of the Holy Spirit" (Romans 15:13 NIV).

So what is hope? A definition I read says, "the feeling that what is wanted can be had or that events will turn out for the best".

I will be honest, sometimes life can be difficult, hard to understand, and all those things we want, and may not show up, the events may not turn out like we planned. So if that is the case, then where and how do we get hope?

Sometimes there can be false hope, misplaced hope, hope that is not founded on God. So where do we go from here? If we have lost hope, how do we get it back?

The first thing we need to do is REALIZE that hope is our ANCHOR!! When the winds and rain of life began to beat down on you and toss you around, put your ANCHOR down. Hope gives you the ability to look on the other side of the storm and know you will make it through. Hope keeps you standing firm when your knees are getting weak.

In the book of Proverbs, we see that when we lose "hope" we can get sick.

"Hope deferred makes the heart sick,
but a longing fulfilled is a tree of life"
(Proverbs 13:12 NIV).

The second thing we need to do is REALIZE that God is our AMAZING source of hope. We have to submit to God, turn over all our anxiety, false hopes, and misplaced hopes. In 1 Peter, we are told to "give God ALL our cares, because He cares for us."

The third thing we need to do is REALIZE that we must ALLOW things to happen on God's timetable. Not ours, or yours, but God's. Sometimes we take off out of the gate, and we run ahead of God, sometimes we run so slow, God is way out in front of us. God will always answer prayer, but we have to wait on His timing. I heard a song some years ago, by Kathy Troccoli and I love the lyrics.

"I've traveled long, I've traveled hard
And stumbled many times along the way
I've bruised my knees a lot
And turned my back on God and seen His mercy

I've been quick to judge and slow to learn
So many times, I've gotten in the way
I think, I know so much
I`ve questioned God enough but still He loves me

So now, I'll walk a different road
I want to see Him there before I even go
I've run ahead and gone too slow
I've got to be still now and wait upon His will now
This time, it's gonna be His time

Don't want to live without the peace
That comes to me when I am by His side
I've known the freedom there
I can't find it anywhere but in Christ Jesus

So now, I'll walk a different road
I want to see Him there before I even go
I've run ahead and gone too slow

I've got to be still now and wait upon His will now
This time, it's gonna be His time

I believe He's got a plan
Everything in His time
I may not always understand
Everything in His time, everything in His time

So now, I'll walk a different road
I want to see Him there before I even go
I've run ahead and gone too slow
I've got to be still now and wait upon His will

So now, I'll walk a different road
I want to see Him there before I even go
I've run ahead and gone too slow
I've got to be still now and wait upon His will now
This time, it's gonna be His time" [17]

The fourth thing we must do is to REALIZE we must praise and thank God ALL the time. Now I know this seems like a hard task. Rejoicing as we are waiting for our hopes to come to fruition is not what we think about doing. Rejoicing enables

God to perfect us in ways we are unable to see at the time.

"By entering through faith into what God has always wanted to do for us—set us right with him, make us fit for him—we have it all together with God because of our Master Jesus. And that's not all: We throw open our doors to God and discover at the same moment that he has already thrown open his door to us. We find ourselves standing where we always hoped we might stand—out in the wide open spaces of God's grace and glory, standing tall and shouting our praise.

There's more to come: We continue to shout our praise even when we're hemmed in with troubles, because we know how troubles can develop passionate patience in us, and how that patience, in turn, forges the tempered steel of virtue, keeping us alert for whatever God will do next. In alert expectancy such as this, we're never left feeling shortchanged. Quite the contrary—we can't round up enough containers to hold everything God generously pours into our lives through the Holy Spirit" *(Romans 5:1-5 MSG)!*

The fifth thing we must do is REALIZE that God's Word is full of promises and ALLOW ourselves to reflect on those. The psalmist wrote in verse 50, "your promises hold me up in the bad times". The Word of God is full of promises from God, and we need to look at the stories of God's faithfulness to one's in the Word and look at others around us.

PROMISES

What are some promises found in God's Word that give you hope or bring comfort when you are having a bad time? What are some promises found in God's Word that gets you excited about living?

What do you think about when you hear these words, anytime and anywhere? God wants all of you, right now, and right where you are. When the **waves of doubt** are **slapping** you in the face, and the **winds of despair** are **slowing** your running pace down, we must look to God's Word and search out the promises He gives.

 We have mentioned it before, but when we are running the race of life we must keep a steady pace. Sometimes it is difficult. I know that when I have gone out running and the wind is blowing hard, it's difficult to keep a good pace.

In Psalms 18 we are told that "God is our rock and our salvation." In Matthew 11, Jesus calls us to "come and rest, for his burdens are not heavy." In Psalms 46 we know that God is our refuge when we are in trouble.

Let's stop a moment and look at it this way. When God gives you a promise, you FIGHT for it. The devil will do anything he can to get you to take your eyes off the promises of God.

God had promised Joshua the Promised Land and God had promised Joshua that wherever the sole of his foot would tread, then that land would be his. But Joshua still had to fight for it and this is what they did. Many times we think that God should just give us our promise on a silver platter. But we must remember that the devil does not want us to walk in the promises of God. In fact, he will try to get you to give up on those promises, so, therefore, we must fight for the promises God has given to us.

Joshua had to go up against giants that were occupying the land. If he simply would have looked at those giants and based his decisions on the circumstances around him, he would have never made it to the Promised Land.

So why don't we claim the promises of God? I suppose it is because we don't like conflict, or we have become lazy, or we don't want to seem weird to others. Fighting takes discipline, fighting involves getting your hands dirty, sometimes fighting is a bloody mess. Christianity is not just a feel-good, warm and fuzzy feeling. If you don't believe me, then take a long hard look at Calvary. Jesus Christ endured the cross for us, so we should be able to stand and fight for Him and His promises. The devil will come at you sometimes in an all- out attack and he will bring hell with him and try to take you out. So we need to stand and fight. When the devil comes in to tell you that you are unworthy, fight back! Stand on the promises of God. When the devil comes and whispers in your ear and tells you to "drop out of the race, turn your back on God" then fight back. Stand on the promises of God.

Ephesians 6 tells us to "put on all of the whole armor of God that He has given us". You don't go into the fight if you are not prepared, you don't go into the fight if you don't have your defense and your offensive weapons ready.

Let's take a look at these:

BELT OF TRUTH (vs. 14)-The belt goes around the waist and it holds all the pieces of the armor together. It secures the outfit and allows the soldier to move freely. Truth secures us and gives us freedom. When we live our lives in truth, honesty and integrity, then the other pieces of armor stay intact.

BREASTPLATE OF RIGHTEOUSNESS (Vs. 14)-The breastplate covers our heart and other vital organs. The breastplate of righteousness covers the most vulnerable areas of the soldier. In the book of Proverbs, we are told to "keep our hearts with all diligence because out of it flows the springs of life." The devil will shoot his arrows right at your heart. We must have it covered with the righteousness of Christ.

FOOTWEAR OF THE READINESS OF THE GOSPEL (VS. 15)-We must have our feet covered and be ready to walk and share the gospel of peace. We should be ready with our feet to flee the devil and walk with God wherever He is ready to send us.

SHIELD OF FAITH (Vs.16)-We know that we believe in Jesus Christ which is our faith. We must continually use this faith to battle the "fiery darts" of the devil. We are able to deflect and extinguish those fiery arrows with our faith.

HELMET OF SALVATION (Vs. 17)-The helmet for a soldier is to protect his head. We should have this helmet on to protect our minds. It is because of the salvation we have received through Jesus Christ our minds can be sound because in the New Testament we are told that we have the mind of Christ.

SWORD OF THE SPIRIT (Vs. 17)-The Word of God is the sword we must use in battle. We have mentioned earlier, that we must memorize the Word and be prepared at all times. We are told in Hebrews that the Word of God is "sharper than any two-edged sword". We are also told in the same verse that the Word of God will "pierce the soul and spirit, joints and marrow, and will discern the thoughts and intentions of the heart."

PRAYING IN THE SPIRIT (Vs. 18)-So many want to leave this out when talking about the armor of God. We have 5 defensive pieces of armor and we have 2 offensive weapons. We have the Word of God which is our sword, but we must use prayer when we go into the battle. Praying in the Spirit letting all our request to be made before God and staying alert.

With God's armor and the Word and prayer, we claim the promises of God. Get dressed, get up and let's fight.

SONG FROM THE HEART

I believe the song here is verse 54. "I set your instructions to music and sing them on my way." We have songs in our HEARTS, we have songs of HOPE, and we have songs of PROMISES. We must continually memorize God's Word and be prepared to stand and fight for the promises of God.

A number of years ago researchers performed an experiment to see the effect hope has on those undergoing hardship. Two sets of laboratory rats were placed in separate tubs of water. The researchers left one set in the water and found that within an hour they had all drowned. The other rats were periodically lifted out of the water and then returned. When that happened, the second set of rats swam for over 24 hours. Why? Not because they were given a rest, but because they suddenly had hope!

Those animals somehow hoped that if they could stay afloat just a little longer, someone would reach down and rescue them. If hope holds such power for unthinking rodents, how much greater should is effect be on our lives. 18

Recently National Geographic *ran an article about the Alaskan Bull Moose. The males of the species battle for dominance during the fall breeding season, literally going head-to-head with antlers crunching together as they collide. Often the antlers, their only weapon are broken. That ensures defeat. The heftiest moose, with the largest and strongest antlers, triumphs. The one that consumes the best diet for growing antlers and gaining weight will be the heavyweight in the fight. Those that eat inadequately sport weaker antlers and less bulk. Therefore, the battles that take place in the fall are won during the summer. There is a lesson here for us. Spiritual battles await. Satan will choose a season to attack. Will we be victorious, or will we fall? Much depends on what we do now—before the wars begin. The bull-moose principle: Enduring faith, strength, and wisdom for trials are best developed before they're needed.* [19]

William Booth the founder of the Salvation Army put these words down about what he knew he needed to do.

"While women weep, as they do now,
I'll fight
While little children go hungry, as they do now,
I'll fight
While men go to prison, in and out, in and out, as they do now,
I'll fight
While there is a drunkard left,
While there is a poor lost girl upon the streets,
While there remains one dark soul without the light of God,
I'll fight-I'll fight to the very end!" [20]

OUR PRAYER

Heavenly Father, we want to thank You for the promises in Your Word that give us hope. We want to always fight for those promises as we put on the armor of God. We thank You for Jesus Christ, Your Son because through Him we have the most wonderful promise and hope of all, peace with You. In Jesus' Name, Amen.

Song #8

"From the Bottom of My Heart"

"I utter this word with deepest affection and from the very bottom of my heart."[21]
Giuseppe Garibaldi

Psalms 119:57-64

57 Thou art my portion, O LORD: I have said that I would keep thy words.

58 I intreated thy favour with my whole heart: be merciful unto me according to thy word.

59 I thought on my ways, and turned my feet unto thy testimonies.

60 I made haste, and delayed not to keep thy commandments.

61 The bands of the wicked have robbed me: but I have not forgotten thy law.

62 At midnight I will rise to give thanks unto thee because of thy righteous judgments.

63 I am a companion of all them that fear thee, and of them that keep thy precepts.

[64]The earth, O LORD, is full of thy mercy: teach me thy statutes."

Earlier in this book, we looked at the words the psalmist used when he asked God to "deal bountifully with him." Once again we see the psalmist throwing out the same kind of phrase when he says "be gracious to me". We will explore this idea a little later in this chapter.

When we look at the quote above we notice Guiseppe Garibaldi had used a phrase or a word and whoever he said it to, he said it from the "bottom of his heart." Guiseppe Garibaldi was a soldier who had become an Italian General and was used greatly in bringing unification to Italy. Some have cited that he was a Christian, but he practiced it on more of an individualistic way. He did not care much for the church. The quote above came from a speech he was giving in 1860 when he addressed his fellow soldiers and was eloquently calling them to "arms" and believing that the oppressors of Italy would disappear.

In the last chapter, we discussed God's promises and a need to stand and fight for those promises.

So we are called to put on our armor and pick up our weapons and fight the battle from the bottom of our hearts.

The Hebrew letter associated with this section of verses is the letter **HETH**. The meaning of this letter some have the belief that it means to "fence in" or "destroy". Sometimes in the naming of the letter they often looked at the design and believe this also could mean to "stack stones".

Vs. 57-You Lord are my
    PORTION, I
    PROMISE to obey Your Word.

Vs. 58-I am
    BEGGING You from the
    BOTTOM of my heart, therefore
    BE gracious to me.

Vs. 59-I have
    TAKEN into consideration my ways, I have
    TURNED my
    STEPS to Your
    STATUTES.

Vs. 60-I will not
DELAY or
DRAG my feet, I obey your commands.

Vs. 61-The
WICKED tie me up, and there is no
WAY out, I will not forget Your
WORD.

Vs. 62-RISING at midnight to thank You for Your
RIGHTEOUS Word.

Vs. 63-I am a
FRIEND to those who
FEAR You and to those who
FOLLOW Your Word.

Vs. 64-Your
LOVE fills the earth, teach me to
LIVE by Your Word.

SATISFIED

According to what version or translation you are reading from verse 57 uses the word "portion". Another translation uses the word "satisfaction."

In today's language and the world, we do not hear the word "portion" aside from food. The word portion is mentioned quite frequently in the Old Testament and can refer to someone's share in a meal, part of a sacrifice, soldiers share in the plunder or someone's inheritance. The word is used 159 times in the Word of God. Many times in Psalms the word is used in accordance with God.

Have you ever thought of God as your "portion"?

Honestly, I have read it many times, but I have not really taken the time to consider its meaning when it comes to God. In Psalms 73, we read the psalm written by Asaph.

Asaph was one of David's musicians. He was a composer of music. Asaph was also the founder of a school of music. He is the writer of several psalms. He conducted the music in the tent when the ark was taken to Jerusalem. In verse 12 of the 73rd psalm, Asaph tells about the wicked and their prosperity then in verse 16 through 18 Asaph seems to understand the final destination of the wicked. He portrays the wicked as people who are running up a muddy hill and it is a slippery slope and eventually, they will be swept away. Later in verse 26, Asaph recognizes that it doesn't matter how much the wicked prosper because his portion is not of this earth, but God.

In verse 26, he talks about God being his portion forever. Still when we read the word portion it just seems foreign to us, because we do not use the word much today. When God is our portion, we must realize that He alone is what satisfies. Each time we stop and think about God being our portion, we must be reminded that whatever happens in this world, we have a satisfaction, a portion, a possession that exceeds and will outshine all of our trials, all tragedies, and any difficulty we might encounter. We are living in the world that is filled with trouble and violence and sometimes it is easy to become discouraged with circumstances we face.

We must think more in the terms of what I just talked about!! We must practice and realize that when we have God, we don't need anything else. He alone is our portion, He alone is our satisfaction.

GRACE

At the beginning of this chapter, we noticed the psalmist was asking for "favor" or "grace" from God depending on what version you might be reading. The three versions that I have in front of me all use the word "graciousness." So here is my question. Is it okay to ask God for favor or grace? Before we answer that question let's spend a little time looking at the word "grace".

Sometimes I believe the word grace is overly used in our culture and our churches. I also believe that sometimes we always want to talk about grace in our churches, but we really don't live grace. I also believe at times we really don't understand the magnitude of God's grace for us. His grace is so BIG, and so DEEP, and WIDE, I think it is hard for us to completely grasp the whole idea of God's grace. When we are talking about grace I think it will help us understand it even more if we spend a little time talking about the different types of grace that are presented throughout God's Word.

COMMON GRACE would be the first one I would like to draw our attention to. God loves all people.

So, therefore, common grace is what He gives to all of us whether we believe in Him or not.

"This is what God does. He gives his best—the sun to warm and the rain to nourish—to everyone, regardless: the good and bad, the nice and nasty" (Matthew 5:45 MSG).

SAVING GRACE is the second one we will want to look at. This is the one that is talked about by most Christians and churches. This is the grace that deals with salvation. This grace is where God sent His only Son Jesus to die on a cross for our sins, and bestows upon us through salvation by faith when we accept His gift. This grace is an overwhelming thought.

"For it is by grace you have been saved, through faith—and this is not from yourselves, it is the gift of God" (Ephesians 2:8 NIV).

SANCTIFYING GRACE is where we are headed next. Right after we have this saving grace, then God's power begins to work in our lives to purify us and to sanctify us. I think sometimes when we hear the word "sanctify" we have a tendency to think of someone who thinks they are better than everyone else. When in reality sanctify, simply means to be "set apart". When we are obedient to God we start the process of sanctifying grace because we have begun the purification process, but ultimately God is the one that we must count on His sanctifying grace.

"Being confident of this, that he who began a good work in you will carry it on to completion until the day of Christ Jesus" (Philippians 1:6 NIV).

PROVISIONAL GRACE is the fourth grace we are looking at. When you get a better job or an unexpected gift we can count those things as a gift of grace from God. Provisional grace is the grace that God will supply all of our needs. I love the way this next verse talks about God's provisional grace.

"Every desirable and beneficial gift comes out of heaven. The gifts are rivers of light cascading down from the Father of Light. There is nothing deceitful in God, nothing two-faced, nothing fickle" (James 1:17 MSG).

SERVING GRACE is bestowed upon each of us. Every believer is given some spiritual gifts and with those gifts, we SERVE and STRENGTHEN other believers. Maybe it is the gift of giving, teaching, preaching, singing, or writing, whatever your gifts are then you serve with those gifts.

"Each of you should use whatever gift you have received to serve others, as faithful stewards of God's grace in its various forms" (1 Peter 4:10 NIV).

SUSTAINING GRACE is the next one that I will write about. When we face trials or suffering then we are given sustaining grace. What helps us keep it all together when we are burdened with death, sickness, and troubles; it is God and His grace that sustains us.

"But he said to me, "My grace is sufficient for you, for my power is made perfect in weakness." Therefore I will boast all the more gladly about my weaknesses, so that Christ's power may rest on me" (2 Corinthians 12:9 NIV).

"Let us then approach God's throne of grace with confidence, so that we may receive mercy and find grace to help us in our time of need" (Hebrews 4:16 NIV).

Different types of grace, but all given by God, and all are without limit. Now that we have looked at different types of grace, let us go backward and look at the question I asked earlier and see if we can find an answer. Do you think it is right for a Christian to ask God for grace or favor?

Let us go back to what the psalmist wrote in this chapter. I am going to put this in my own words. The psalmist says, "I have sought you Lord from the bottom of my heart, so give me favor, give me grace according to Your Word." Notice what is said when He is asking God to be gracious, he also states "according to Your Word." So is it right to ask for favor? If we ask in alignment with God's Word. Let's look at what the Bible says about asking.

7 "Ask and it will be given to you; seek and you will find; knock and the door will be opened to you. 8 For everyone who asks receives; the one who seeks finds; and to the one who knocks, the door will be opened.

9 "Which of you, if your son asks for bread, will give him a stone? 10 Or if he asks for a fish, will give him a snake? 11 If you, then, though you are evil, know how to give good gifts to your children, how much more will your

Father in heaven give good gifts to those who ask him" (Matthew 7:7-11 NIV)!

According to the verses in Matthew, we can ask God, seek out God, and even knock on His door. If we ask we receive, because God gives good gifts to those who ask. God's grace is a good gift. Let's look at the other side of this thought though in reference to the "graces" mentioned above. We are all given common grace, sometimes we don't use it, but we do have it. Saving grace is something I don't believe we need to ask for, because in the book of Romans it tells us that if we believe that Jesus was crucified, and believe that He arose from the dead, and we profess it and call upon the Lord's name, then we are a Christian. We don't really need to ask for sanctifying grace because we know that He is working in us until the day we arrive in Heaven when His work in us is completed. We don't need to ask for provisional grace, even though we do, the Word of God tells us "He supplies all of our needs". This is not a debate it is a statement telling us that He will. We don't need to ask for serving grace, most of us are able to serve, we have gifts we can use, and we just need to use them. Last, we don't need to ask for God to sustain us through the hard times, even though many times we pray for strength and we pray that he will help us through a circumstance, but when you really look at this, Hebrews just tells us to go to the throne of grace, and we will receive mercy and grace in the time of need.

When we pause a moment and reflect on the previous pages that have already been written and have already been read, we realize that these "graces" mentioned above are all promises. These promises are all found in the Word of God and so if we ask for favor or grace then we must use the words "according to Your Word."

One other thing I want to add about grace. I have a CD here at the house, and there is one song in particular that I listen to 3 or 4 times a day. The CD is titled "New Grace", and the song has the same name. As I have listened to this many times over, I began to wonder in my own mind if there was such a thing as "dying grace." This would be grace given to us at the time of our departure from this earth. You will be able to read the lyrics below, but you will have to buy the CD and notice how wonderful the song is.

Read the following lyrics and then I will talk about "dying grace".

"All of grace that's my story all the way from earth to glory,
Since by grace, he lifted me from sin and woe!
Living grace he has extended, eyes on him my heart depended,
He'll give new grace when it's my time to go!

Grace not yet discovered, grace not yet uncovered,
Grace from his bountiful store.
Grace to cross the river, Grace to face forever,
There'll be new grace I've not needed before.

There's been grace for every mile, there's been grace for every trial,
There's been grace sufficient from his vast supply.
Grace to make my life more tender,
Grace to love and pray for sinners,
There'll be new grace when it's time to die! [22]

Look at the first and the second line of the song, it talks of the Saving Grace, and then the third line talks of the Sanctifying Grace. The chorus echoes the sentiments of a new grace given when we die. Look at the second verse of this song and you will see the other graces already mentioned. The songwriter talks of Sustaining Grace in the first line. Then he goes on and talks about Provisional Grace in the next line. Then in the next two lines, he finishes my thoughts and his by talking about Serving Grace. Then once again he talks about a new grace given to us as we cross over to the other side.

When I heard this song, I was literally blown away especially when I started writing this chapter. So let's take a little time and cover the next grace.

DYING GRACE is the last one I would like to talk about. I am not trying to paint a dark and grim picture, I am taking the "grace" brush and dipping it in the brightest colors because for a Christian death should be glorious.

We all will die one day and we do not know the when or how. Some of us will die painfully, some peacefully, and some with honor. Some will simply fall asleep to only awaken on the other side. Some will lose their life fighting on the battlefield. However one dies, we know that for the Christian, God wants you and me to realize that death is not a fearful thing but a wonderful event. God and His wonderful grace have supplied it through your life, so He will continue to supply it even through the death experience.

I could write a whole chapter on death and dying grace, but I won't. To the unbeliever death is a fearful thing. For the believer, we can look at it like the song above says, "there will be new grace when it's my time to go."

In the book of Isaiah and in the 30th chapter, Isaiah tells us "the Lord longs to be gracious". This grace is from here on earth all the way to glory.

COMMANDS/ADVICE

How quickly do you obey God's commands? When you read the Word of God do you see it as ADVICE or do you read it as COMMANDS. Many times I believe and think that many Christians read the Word and consider the words they read as advice, something they can do or not do.

Anywhere we look in the world we can find someone who wants to give us some advice. We might be the kind of person that likes giving advice. But advice is simply defined as "an opinion or suggestion of what someone should do".

Sometimes we don't like people's advice, and sometimes we might consider their advice. I have daughters who are now married and when they or their husband is trying to make a decision about something, sometimes I or my wife will give them advice on what we think they should do. They have two options, disregard the advice or use the advice. Because the advice I am giving just might be my opinion, and it simply might be a suggestion. It is not a command to do.

People have a tendency to look at the Word of God the same way. We have a tendency; I'm using the term "we" not meaning everyone, to look at God's Word as advice. Sometimes we read it and then walk away and sometimes we do what He commands and sometimes we don't, I believe it is because we consider His word more of an advice book.

The things we read in God's Word, like loving our neighbor, is not a suggestion or a piece of advice it is a command. When we are told to "love the Lord God with all our hearts, souls, minds, and strength, it is not a suggestion of doing it only if we think it is good advice, it is a command.

The psalmist writes, "I will not delay in obeying Your commands". Do we delay?

SONG FROM THE HEART

The song here is found in verse 58 when the psalmist prays for favor with all of his heart. We have covered all of this in this chapter. In this chapter, I used the words "bottom of my heart." Whether we use "all" or "bottom of" we encompass the whole heart. Many times the phrase "all my heart" is mentioned in the Bible. We should be seeking God, learning His Word, reading His Word, and obeying Him with "all of our hearts."

In 1891, Salvation Army Captain Joseph McFee was distraught because so many poor individuals in San Francisco were going hungry. During the holiday season, he resolved to provide a free Christmas dinner for the destitute and poverty-stricken. He only had one major hurdle to overcome – funding the project.

Where would the money come from, he wondered. He lay awake nights, worrying, thinking, and praying about how he could find the funds to fulfill his commitment of feeding 1,000 of the city's poorest individuals on Christmas Day. As he pondered the issue, his thoughts drifted back to his sailor days in Liverpool, England. He remembered how at Stage Landing, where the boats came in, there was a large, iron kettle called "Simpson's Pot" into which passers-by tossed a coin or two to help the poor.

The next day Captain McFee placed a similar pot at the Oakland Ferry Landing at the foot of Market Street. Beside the pot, he placed a sign that read, "Keep the Pot Boiling." He soon had the money to see that the needy people were properly fed at Christmas.

Six years later, the kettle idea spread from the west coast to the Boston area. That year, the combined effort nationwide resulted in 150,000 Christmas dinners for the needy. In 1901, kettle contributions in New York City provided funds for the first mammoth sit-down dinner in Madison Square Garden, a custom that continued for many years. Today in the U.S., The Salvation Army assists more than four-and-a-half million people during the Thanksgiving and Christmas time periods.

Captain McFee's kettle idea launched a tradition that has spread not only throughout the United States but all across the world. Kettles are now used in such distant lands as Korea, Japan, Chile and many European countries. Everywhere, public contributions to Salvation Army kettles enable the organization to continue its year-round efforts at helping those who would otherwise be forgotten. [23]

The founder of the Salvation Army was William Booth. He converted to Methodism as a young adult and was a fervent believer in evangelical Christianity. The Salvation Army spread to become a global humanitarian charity seeking to provide material aid and spiritual salvation. Here us what William Booth said about starting the Salvation Army.

"I will tell you the secret: God has had all that there was of me. There have been men with greater brains than I, even with greater opportunities, but from the day I got the poor of London on my heart and caught a vision of what Jesus Christ could do with me and them, on that day I made up my mind that God should have all of William Booth there was. And if there is anything of power in the Salvation Army, it is because God has had all the adoration of my heart, all the power of my will, and all the influence of my life."[24]

William Booth made such a remarkable impact on the people of his day that over 150,000 people filed by his casket while over 40,000 people attended his funeral.

William Booth did all that he did from the "bottom of his heart".

OUR PRAYER

Heavenly Father, we pray that we will use the grace You so freely bestow upon us. Help us to constantly look at Your Word and obey the commands that you give to us. In Jesus' Name, Amen.

Song #9

"For the Best"

"Sometimes you just have to stop worrying, wondering and doubting. Have faith that things will work out maybe not how you planned, but just how they're meant to be."[25]
Author Unknown

Psalms 119:65-72

[65] *"Thou hast dealt well with thy servant, O Lord, according unto thy word.*

[66] *Teach me good judgment and knowledge: for I have believed thy commandments.*

[67] *Before I was afflicted I went astray: but now have I kept thy word.*

[68] *Thou art good, and doest good; teach me thy statutes.*

[69] *The proud have forged a lie against me: but I will keep thy precepts with my whole heart.*

[70] *Their heart is as fat as grease; but I delight in thy law.*

[71] *It is good for me that I have been afflicted; that I might learn thy statutes.*

72 The law of thy mouth is better unto me than thousands of gold and silver."

Sufferings, afflictions, trouble all seem to come our way. Sometimes these things are from an outside source, something we have no control over. Sometimes these things are brought on by our own decisions. The psalmist uses the word "afflicted" twice in these eight verses. In verse 67, he says, "I strayed then I was "afflicted" giving the connotation that it was something that he had done to bring about this trouble. In verse 72 he is glad that he has been in trouble or afflicted, giving the idea that these afflictions came from an outside source. In verse 69, he tells us that the "arrogant are telling lies". We will take a deeper look at these thoughts here in just a moment.

The 9th letter of the Hebrew alphabet is **TETH**. Believed this letter derived from *twh*, which means "spin" *Teth* brings the idea of knot, or knotted, to interweave, or to twist into each other. The shape of this letter gives the idea of a vortex.

Vs. 65- Be
GOOD to your servant, be
GOOD just like your Word.

Vs. 66-TEACH me common sense, for I
TRUST in Your Word.

Vs. 67-Before my
AFFLICTIONS I went
ASTRAY, now I obey Your Word.

Vs. 68-You Lord are
GOOD, and the source of
GOOD, teach me Your
GOODNESS.

Vs. 69-The
ARROGANT tell lies about me, but my
ATTENTION   on Your Word, I give with
ALL of myself.

Vs. 70-Their hearts are
COLD and
CALLOUSED, they are
BORING and
BLAND, but I
DELIGHT in Your
DECREES.

Vs. 71-My
>TROUBLES
>TURNED out for the best. Your
>TEXTBOOK is what I learn from.

Vs. 72-TRUTH from Your
>MOUTH is
>MORE precious than
>THOUSANDS of pieces of silver and gold

SUFFERING BECAUSE OF "US"

We have mentioned it earlier, but sometimes we bring about afflictions or suffering from the bad decisions we make. When we make a wrong choice or a bad decision, then we must face the consequences of those decisions and sometimes we will have to suffer for it. Sometimes we have to endure the painful consequences in order to understand the joy that comes with living in accordance to God's Word. Just like when you warn your child over and over not to touch the hot stove, and they still do and they get burned, they will suffer a painful consequence. We, many times are like those children and we go against what God says, or we stray, and when we do we will suffer the painful consequences. The psalmist in verse 67 obviously had walked down this road.

One of the reasons I believe the author of Psalms 119 is King David is because of verse 67 and verse 71. King David had faced many "afflictions" and some of these were brought on by his own actions. David knew what it was like to stray. How about ourselves? Do we venture out on our own and when we do we suffer? Let's take a look at a man who suffered and paid the consequences because of his own self-inflictions and afflictions.

JACOB

Jacob was full of self-affliction. The first thing we notice is that he lied to his own father. Some will say that since it was told by God that Jacob would be the one that was blessed, then it was alright to lie. But as we will see here in just a moment, lying to his father brought about consequences. Think about this for a moment. The way you treat your parents may come back to haunt you. Maybe your parents have passed on, but the memories still hang around.

Second, Jacob cheated his brother. He cheated him out of his inheritance and blessing. His consequence is that he lived in fear of his brother for 20 years. This memory of cheating haunted him for 20 years.

Third, Jacob failed to be a proper example for his children. He allowed them to have other idols. His children became murderers. His children took one of their own brothers and sold him into slavery.

Look at the painful consequences that Jacob had to face. He cheated his family, his family cheated him. His father-in-law had him work for more years than promised and he eventually married Rachel the one he loved. He lied to his family, and his family lied to him. They sold their brother into slavery, and took his "coat of many colors", and told their father that Joseph had died. He suffered tremendously because he lost his home when he lied, he lost his sons to selfishness, he lost his son because of lying, he lost a wife in childbirth, and he lost a son because of his own sorrow.

Take a look at your life while I take a look at my own. Have we lied to a parent, a child or a friend? Have we cheated? Are we being the right kind of example? We have to look at our lives, are we cheating people? Are we great examples to our children?

When we make bad decisions or bring suffering to ourselves because of something we have done or not done, the Lord our Heavenly Father still has to deal with us. When you send warnings to your children about certain decisions they make, there are times when we have to discipline those children for the bad decisions they made. God has to do that with His children as well.

"And have you completely forgotten this word of encouragement that addresses you as a father addresses his son? It says,

"My son, do not make light of the Lord's discipline,
*   and do not lose heart when he rebukes you,*
⁶ because the Lord disciplines the one he loves,
*   and he chastens everyone he accepts as his son." ⁷ Endure hardship as discipline; God is treating you as his children. For what children are not disciplined by their*

father? ⁸ If you are not disciplined—and everyone undergoes discipline—then you are not legitimate, not true sons and daughters at all. ⁹ Moreover, we have all had human fathers who disciplined us and we respected them for it. How much more should we submit to the Father of spirits and live!¹⁰ They disciplined us for a little while as they thought best; but God disciplines us for our good, in order that we may share in his holiness. ¹¹ No discipline seems pleasant at the time, but painful. Later on, however, it produces a harvest of righteousness and peace for those who have been trained by it" (Hebrews 12:5-11 NIV).

Sometimes we bring trouble to ourselves, and sometimes it comes from an outside source.

SUFFERING FROM OUTSIDE

We suffer from things that come our way and we have no control over certain things. Sometimes it might be our health, it might be in losing our wealth, and it might even be the death of a loved one or a friend. Most churches that I have attended and most churches, in general, avoid the topic of suffering as though it is a plague. Human nature itself longs for comfort and peace. We as humans avoid suffering at any cost. I don't want to suffer and I don't know anyone who desires to suffer. We know that suffering is a part of life, and we need Christians and churches that are ready and willing to prepare and equip believers to expect to suffer.

Some of the suffering we may experience might just be for a short time, but there are times when certain afflictions or suffering might last a few months or maybe even years. It is one thing to have to deal with some affliction for a day, or a week, and maybe even a month. But it is a far greater burden to bear when the suffering goes on for months or years.

JOB

One day Satan was walking around on the earth looking at all the servants of God and he noticed Job. He was an upright, good standing, righteous man, that feared God and abstained from evil. So God and Satan were talking back and forth, and Satan said, "This Job guy has it easy, does he fear You because he is a good guy?" He continued, "I bet if you took away everything he has, he will turn around and curse you to your face." God replied, "Go ahead, do anything you want to him, just don't kill him." So Satan left the presence of God.

Here is what happens next. Job has seven sons and three daughters and they were all over at the oldest son's house having a party. Now Job was a wealthy guy, he had a big farm, and he owned 7,000 sheep, 3,000 camels, 500 oxen, 500 donkeys and a nice place to live. Looks to me as if he had a zoo, not a farm. So the story continues. The children were having a meal and listening to some music. The servants were outside doing their duties when one servant ran to the house of Job and reported some bad news.

"Job, the oxen were plowing and the donkeys were in the field grazing when the Sabeans attacked. They stole the animals and killed the other servants, I managed to escape." While this servant was talking, another one came running in and said, "bolts of lightning struck the sheep and the shepherds and fried them, and they have all died. I am the only one who escaped." While this guy was still talking, another servant came rushing through the door and said, "The Chaldeans have come from three different directions and they have killed all the camels and the camel drivers. I am the only one who escaped."

Now stop and pause with me for just a moment. Job is in his home and three messengers have all come in and told him that he has lost all his animals. Bad, really bad sufferings.

Let's go on. While these three servants were telling Job of what was going on, here comes a fourth servant and says, "While your children gathered in the house of your oldest son, a tornado came in from the desert and has hit the house and the house collapsed and they have all died. I am the only one to get out alive."

In one day Job lost everything he owned, all of his children. Then right after that, Job developed some kind of disease on his skin.

At the end of chapter one of Job, it tells us that "not one time did Job sin, and not one time did he blame God."

Now you would think, and I would think that Job would be honored for his faithfulness to God right away. But it didn't happen that way. This suffering that Job had to endure went on for months and months. At the end of the book of Job, we see that God restored everything to Job more than what he had before. Why? Job was faithful through all of his sufferings. Look what his restoration included, 14,000 sheep, 6,000 camels, 1,000 oxen, and 1,000 donkeys. He also had more children which were seven sons and three daughters. Job lived another 140 years and he was able to see his grandchildren and their children. Four generations in all.

I don't know about you, but I know if I lost all of my children in one afternoon I would have a very difficult time. So what do we do when we suffer afflictions that are out of our control? What do we do when things don't seem to go our way?

Some of you might be at a certain point right now where you want to give up on God. In your life, it doesn't seem like things are working out.

Maybe you have not received the job you really wanted. Maybe you have lost your job and you are struggling to make ends meet. Maybe you have a terminal illness that you are dealing with and you seem to be in pain every day. I don't know what is going on with you. I pray today that your suffering will only be for a while and not for a great length of days.

Where do we go from here? Suffering at the hands of "us", or suffering from the hands of uncontrollable circumstances, should lead us to Jesus Christ. The psalmist wrote in verse 71, "it was good for me to have afflictions".

When we are under great affliction and great suffering we want it fixed. Many times we spend all of our time trying to figure out why we are going through trials. We as humans have a natural curiosity to know the "Why?" behind what is happening. I know I have, you have too, I am sure. I also have some friends who are an atheist, and they always point to this question. "If God is an all good God, then why is there so much suffering in the world?"

One of the most difficult things to understand or explain is why there is so much pain, suffering, and problems in this life. Sometimes we find ourselves sitting around contemplating "Why?"! If we are not careful we will end up bitter and cynical. If you spend all your time coming up with philosophies of "why" there is suffering, then you are more apt to come to the conclusion like some of my atheist friends that there is no God.

Job had three friends who came to him and began contemplating the reason for Job's suffering and their advice and words only made his agonizing more difficult. Job's wife even wanted Job to "curse God and die!" By the time we get to the end of Job, we see that God revealed to Job that he didn't need to know the reason "Why." Even if God were to explain it to him, I am not sure Job could have understood it.

BETTER OR BITTER

So how do we deal with our sufferings, our afflictions?

First we have to look at our ATTITUDE. I read this the other day about attitude.

"Self-esteem is an attitude toward self. Love is our attitude toward others. Faith is your attitude toward God. Hope is your attitude toward the

future. Forgiveness is your attitude toward the past. Everything revolves around attitude." [26]

When it comes to sufferings and afflictions and lives that are in pain our attitude is one of our most valuable assets. Our attitude determines whether we become BETTER or BITTER. Attitude is simply a choice made by each of us. We have been given by God the ability to choose what our response should be. In the book of James, we are told to "count it all joy" when we face trials.

Second we must do as the psalmist has mentioned in this chapter. We must be ATTENTIVE. We must read God's Word and pay attention to the Word. The psalmist wants to know that his afflictions caused him to turn his attention to God's Word and to learn from God. We need to learn that God has our best in store for us, and we may not see it in the middle of our dire circumstances, but we must rely on God and know that He is looking out for us. The psalmist continues and finishes up this section and tells us that the Word of God is more precious than gold. Oh, may we look at the Word of God in such a manner.

SONG FROM THE HEART

In verse 71, he sings this song "It was good for me to be afflicted, so I will learn Your Word." When afflictions strike, when sufferings come your way and my way, I pray that we will have this song in our heart, that it is GOOD for us. In the darkness of our nights, when things seem most dark for us may we always carry a song in our heart. When we find life difficult and we find it difficult to carry a tune, may we sing with our lips and our hearts, because God will give us a song to sing. Sometimes we will learn the sweetest and best songs in the blackness of trial or suffering.

American pastor and author James H. Brookes told of visiting a friend's house and hearing the music of a bird singing. It was not the ordinary sound of chirping; instead, it resembled the strains of a lovely melody. At first, Brookes didn't know where it was coming from; but when he glanced around the room, he saw a beautiful bullfinch in a birdcage. The lady of the house explained that it had been taught to sing that way at night. The teacher would repeat the notes time and again until the bird was able to mimic them. But this was possible only because it was dark and the bird's attention would not be diverted. [27]

OUR PRAYER

Heavenly Father, forgive us when we walk away from You or stray. Teach us through our suffering, even when we make a bad decision and we will thank you for teaching us. Help us to see Your Word and to see it more valuable than anything else we can attain. In Jesus Name, Amen.

Song #10

"The Tune I Dance To"

"Life's not about waiting for the storm to pass. It's about learning to dance in the rain!" **28**
Vivian Greene

Psalms 119:73-80

[73] *"Thy hands have made me and fashioned me: give me understanding, that I may learn thy commandments.*

[74] *They that fear thee will be glad when they see me; because I have hoped in thy word.*

[75] *I know, O LORD, that thy judgments are right, and that thou in faithfulness hast afflicted me.*

[76] *Let, I pray thee, thy merciful kindness be for my comfort, according to thy word unto thy servant.*

[77] *Let thy tender mercies come unto me, that I may live: for thy law is my delight.*

[78] *Let the proud be ashamed; for they dealt perversely with me without a cause: but I will meditate in thy precepts.*

⁷⁹ Let those that fear thee turn unto me, and those that have known thy testimonies.

⁸⁰ Let my heart be sound in thy statutes; that I be not ashamed."

I am sure you have heard the quote above many times. I know I have. We just finished the last chapter by looking at suffering and learning from the writer of Psalms 119 that we should believe it is good for us when those things come our way. The writer of the quotation above believes the very same thing. Sometimes we have to dance in the middle of the suffering, affliction. Sometimes we want to hide when the storms of life come, but we should just run out and dance in the rain. The psalmist presents to us the idea of dancing to the tune of God's Word, delighting in it. I know we have talked about finding delight in God's Word already, but I want to look at it a little differently in this section. Later we will see why the psalmist writes "Your Word is the tune I dance to."

The 10ᵗʰ letter of the Hebrew alphabet is **YOD**. This letter gives us the idea of a hand or a fist. Typically mentioned as the smallest letter in the alphabet, but yet carries the idea of power and might. Some are reminded of a fist because of the shape.

Vs. 73-Your hands formed
    ME, so breathe on
    ME the
    WISDOM of your
    WORD.

Vs. 74-May those who fear you,
    HAVE joy when they see me, for I
    HAVE put my
    HOPE in your Word.

Vs. 75-I know
    LORD, that your
    LAWS are right, Your
    TESTING me has always been
    TRUE and right.

Vs. 76-I take comfort in
    YOUR unfailing love, according to
    YOUR promise to me.

Vs. 77-Your
COMPASSION
COMFORTS me, so I will
DELIGHT and
DANCE to the tune of your Word.

Vs. 78-The arrogant is put to shame for
WRONGING me
WITHOUT cause, I will
MEDITATE with my
MIND on your Word.

Vs. 79-May
THOSE who fear you
TURN to me, may
THEY understand Your Word.

Vs. 80-May I live
WHOLLY and
HOLY with
SOUL and body so I won't be put to
SHAME.

ROLE MODEL

The psalmist prays that he will be a role model for others. He prays that those who honor God would turn to the writer (himself) and rejoice and know God's Word. When we think of role model we think of someone we would admire and want to be like.

I heard a question the other day which asked "Do you consider yourself to be a role model?" Yet we do not need to answer the question with a "yes" or "no" because we already are role models. You may say, "I'm not a role model, I don't want to be one, I don't want that kind of responsibility." The problem with that statement is that you are a role model because someone is watching you, and they are watching me. There is a friend watching you, there is a child watching you, or another family member, and they are all watching how you handle your life, and how you handle your heart. They are watching to see how you handle your family, your wife, your husband, or them.

You are either a positive role model for someone or you are a negative role model. We must evaluate our own life. We must look at our habits. The way we treat people and the way we treat our families will be copied by our children. We learn things from our parents and many times we end up acting just like them.

Role models are always mentioned in the world of sports, entertainment, and music. Younger kids of today want to pattern their lives after some of these role models. Some of these are bad role models and some of them are good.

A recent survey, done by couponcodes4u.com, asked more than 2,000 parents to vote on celebs they felt were negative influences on their children. And it looks like Chris Brown and Miley Cyrus are the king and queen of bad role models!

Unsurprisingly, Chris Brown was voted as the worst male celeb role model in the poll (71%) – probably for beating on-again, off again girlfriend Rihanna back in 2009 – while Miley Cyrus was chosen as the worst female celeb role model (68%) – likely for her transformation from an innocent Disney star to an R-rated personality.

Other female stars who made the naughty list were Lindsay Lohan (65%), Kim Kardashian (63%), Amanda Bynes (61%) and Farrah Abraham (59%).

As for the men, following Chris Brown in the "bad role model" group were Kanye West (67%), Justin Bieber (65%), Lil Wayne (58%) and Charlie Sheen

(56%). Some have gotten arrested, others just have egos the size of Texas – but they all have work to do if they want to be mentors. [29]

I am not going to list the persons or celebrities who would make good role models. I am sure there are many. I can think of a few good names as I am typing. I also think we are in a sad state of affairs in life when the only people we think are role models are either celebrities, sports figures or some musician. The psalmist wanted people to look at him because he had put his hope in God's Word. We need to look at that pattern and find people who rely on and have hope in God's Word and use them as our role models. Pastors, teachers, parents and grandparents who hold tight to the Word of God are the ones we should want to emulate.

So what makes a good role model?

First this role model should REJECT EVIL. We must find people who are not living their life merely by their words, but by their words and their actions. We need role models who live by the verse in the Bible that says "examine everything carefully, hold tight to what is good, and reject every kind of evil."

Second this role model should RIGHTLY DIVIDE THE WORD. We should be smart, knowledgeable about the Word. I have a friend who calls himself an atheist and his claim is that Christians do not know their Bibles because they don't read their Bibles. We should be students of the Word of God. The psalmist prayed that people would look at him, because of his hope in the Word and because that Word is alive and active in his life.

Third this role model should be READY FOR SERVICE. We should be ready and willing to serve. I want to put it down in this book like my son-in-law did in his sermon this past Sunday.

"Our goal should be to LIVE, LOVE, and SERVE like Jesus because that's WHO I am, and that's WHAT I do." [30]

Fourth this role model should REMAIN FAITHFUL. We are to stick to it and stick with it. We are to live in Christ and to endure in Christ by equipping ourselves every day through the Word. We should stay true to whatever task God has for us.

I read an article today about good and bad role models, taken from "The Montana Standard" written by Bill Foley. In this article, he talked about another guy who had written about Jay Cutler. He ended up writing the article about people he thought would be good or bad role models. In the article, he mentioned that it might be better if your kid didn't pick a professional athlete to be his role model. He then went on to say that more than likely they would anyway so he presents a list of some athletes that he figured would be good and bad role models. Here is what he said.

"Good role model: Mairissa Peoples.

The former Butte Central basketball player is facing yet another battle with cancer.

Still, she sure looked like the toughest person in the Butte Civic Center last Thursday night during the Butte High-Butte Central basketball games. She was upbeat and positive as she heads off to kick cancer's butt one last time.

Bad role models: The Butte High fans who left the game early because their team was losing.

Good role model: Warrick Dunn.

163

The former NFL running back's "Homes for the Holidays" foundation furnishes and pays the down payment for new homes for single parents. He recently celebrated the foundation's 100th home.

Bad role model: Ben Roethlisberger.

Good role model: Walter Payton.

Seriously, even though he's no longer with us, there's never been a better role model than the man they called "Sweetness."

Bad role model: Barry Bonds.

The guy treated teammates, fans and media members like garbage. Plus he cheated.

Good role model: Jay Cutler.

He bought Christmas presents for a bunch of sick kids and he didn't do it for the publicity.

One national columnist thinks that's a bad thing. One national columnist has clearly lost his mind.

Bad role model: Aaron Rodgers.

The Packers quarterback soured one of the all-time games played by a quarterback in the playoffs by snubbing a cancer patient looking for an autograph outside the locker room Saturday in Atlanta.

Sure, I was going to give Rodgers the benefit of the doubt when I read about this. Then I saw the video of Rodgers going out of his way to turn the cold shoulder to Jan Cavanaugh, who you could clearly tell was a cancer patient even if she wasn't wearing the pink Packers outfit that highlighted the pink breast cancer ribbon.

Barry Bonds wouldn't have even done that."[31]

There are many others who would make good role models and there are plenty who wouldn't. When we are picking the people we would like to emulate, we must choose wisely. I am sure there are great musicians, and great athletes, who are wonderful role models, but based on the criteria mentioned above how do they compare?

Maybe your role model is a mom, or a dad, or a teacher, or a pastor. Maybe you want to be a role model. Whichever the case may be, make sure we pick them based on their life and not based upon what they do.

Steve DeVore has built a multi-million dollar company on the principle of role modeling.

DeVore is president of Syber Vision, a company that markets instructional video and audio tapes on everything from golf to skiing to weight control. This is not some kind of mystical New Age approach to learning, but rather the master-apprentice relationship put to work in different settings.

When DeVore was in college, he happened to watch a bowling tournament on television. As he paid close attention to the movements of the bowlers, the thought struck him that if he could emulate their movements, he could probably achieve the same results.

After watching the bowlers closely for thirty minutes, he got in his car and drove to the local bowling alley. He got an alley, picked out a ball, and for the next thirty minutes, he did just as the professional bowlers had done on TV. He threw nine straight strikes and recorded a score of 278. His highest score up to that point was 163. By emulating a proficient role model, he improved his performance by 115 pins. But the key was *"just as."* He had to do it just as the pros. 32

IT'S TIME TO DANCE

I won't get into the subject of dancing and whether you or I believe it is right or wrong. I can't dance so that usually makes my mind up pretty quick.

The Bible says, "King David danced before God, with all of his might." When I read that phrase, I picture in my mind, that David was so passionate about the Lord, and so excited about God, that he could not help but dance.

The psalmist (possibly David) wrote that he was so delighted with God's Word, that the Word was the tune he danced to.

What is the tune you are dancing to? Are you even dancing?

Remember the title of this book, "The Singing Traveler". Here you have the author of Psalms 119, singing as he traveled from place to place, and all the words that have been penned down on the pages as he traveled showed that he prayed and many times they came out as songs from the heart. When I started writing this book, I couldn't help but notice that the "traveler", or pilgrim was singing and I am pretty sure in his travels he probably danced a little as well.

Dancing is universal. There are many who are dancing all over the world today and for many different reasons. Some dance to express their emotions, to entertain, to educate and to attract others, or maybe even bring good fortune. Some dance in joy and in celebration, but some dances are associated with anger, protest and war. For centuries, certain dances have been connected with religion, worship and some form of magic. Some dances around the world convey life changes such as births, marriage and sometimes death. My wife and I sit and watch the show "Dancing With the Stars" and usually in the beginning of the season, some of the celebrities just can't dance, and some start to learn and dance well, and some don't make it very far in the competition. Some dances are very technical, but other dances are very emotional.

Two things I see about dancing when I read the above scripture. Our first dance lesson DEPENDING ON GOD. The psalmist had written in the previous section about keeping his focus on

God. If we are dancing, we don't need to dance for the world, we need to dance to God's tune, by depending totally on God. We need to let God give us the tune to dance to. Look at it this way, we have a great God, who has written the music for us, and God has choreographed the dance for you.

Our second dance lesson is to DEEPEN OURSELVES IN THE WORD. I just mentioned it, but look at the Word of God as you would a symphony, a sheet of music, a chorus that we sing to, but we also are able to dance to. God has given us so much in the Word, and the psalmist prays that God will comfort him so he can live because he is dancing to the tune of God's Word. The pages and words of the Bible should be "music to our ears", and we should be ready to learn the music, and then get up and dance to that music.

SONG FROM THE HEART

The writer's song is found in verse 74 and 77, wanting others to see him and rejoice because his hope is in the Word. Also, knowing that he can't live without God and God's Word is his music that he is dancing to.

Do others see God in you? Do others see that you are dancing to God's tune?

I grew up in a household where we didn't dance. I am not sure for the reason of this other than we attended a conservative Baptist church. I think dancing in my family was ranked close to the top of the lists of sins, probably somewhere between murder and robbing a bank.

I really never thought about dancing much as I got older, since I didn't practice it on a regular basis, I never really wanted to dance and never attained any good dance moves. My wife, on the other hand, grew up in a family who danced. So after my kids were born, thank goodness, they all received the dancing genes from their mother.

Over the last number of years, we have always held a "new year's eve party" at our house. My two daughters would invite many of their friends and my son would invite some friends, and usually after the New Year had arrived, they would all turn on the television and put on some music and would spend a few hours dancing. We also would sit around playing games with all of them and their friends. Now I would join in with the dancing because it was fun and I can't dance. I never have a clue what to do, so I just do the best I can.

Two and half years ago I danced with my youngest daughter at her wedding, and then about 2 months ago, I danced with my oldest daughter at her wedding. Those were some of the greatest dancing times I have ever had, even though I still do not know how to dance or have a clue about dancing. I still don't think I am ready for the reality show "So You Think You Can Dance".

I have never wanted people to see me dance, especially people I didn't know. It is also crazy to think that I am a musician and have some kind of rhythm, I would be able to dance, but for some reason, I just can't seem to get the knack of it.

The Message Bible translates the verse "delighted" in the Word, to "dancing to the tune" of the Word. I actually like how the Message Bible puts it because I have never thought of it in the terms of dancing. The psalmist wrote that he wanted people to see him because of his hope in the Word, and understanding of the Word. Since he loved the Word of God so much, he sang about it and danced to it. Since there are people watching us all the time, we should let them see our dancing, our delight, and our hope in the Word of God. At the end of this section of verses, the writer says that he follows the Word of God with all of his heart so that he wouldn't be put to shame.

Our goal should be to find great role models that inspire us to live better, role models that imitate the life of Christ. Our goal should be to follow, dance, sing, and live the Word of God so that we will not be ashamed of God.

OUR PRAYER

Heavenly Father, help us to follow You over everyone else, but also help us to find role models that model God. Help us to dance to the tune of Your Word, and to always know we have hope in You. In Jesus Name, Amen.

Song #11

"Smoke in My Eyes"

"Black and white are the colors of photography.
To me, they symbolize the alternatives of hope
and despair to which mankind is forever
subjected."[33]
Robert Frank

Psalms 119:81-88

[81] *"My soul fainteth for thy salvation: but I
hope in thy word.*

[82] *Mine eyes fail for thy word, saying, When
wilt thou comfort me?*

[83] *For I am become like a bottle in the smoke;
yet do I not forget thy statutes.*

[84] *How many are the days of thy servant? When
wilt thou execute judgment on them that
persecute me?*

[85] *The proud have digged pits for me, which
are not after thy law.*

[86] *All thy commandments are faithful: they
persecute me wrongfully; help thou me.*

[87] *They had almost consumed me upon earth;
but I forsook not thy precepts.*

88 Quicken me after thy lovingkindness; so shall I keep the testimony of thy mouth."

I have stood around campfires many times, and maybe you have as well. In my younger days, when my dad was able to burn limbs and tree clippings, I would stand around and watch the fire because I was intrigued with the flames. Many times he caught me throwing things in the flames. Also, when the wind would start to blow, sometimes the smoke would be blown right into my eyes and they would burn. If you have ever stood around a fire then you probably have had the same experience as me.

In the King James Version verse 83, the writer says that he has become "like a bottle in the smoke". In the Message Version the writer says, "There's smoke in my eyes, they burn and water." Standing around the fire that my dad had started outside, there were times when I would throw in the old soda bottle because I wanted to see what would happen. When the fire had been put out, then next day I would go out and pick up that old bottle and examine it to see how it fared in the fire and the smoke, and every time the bottle would be covered with black smoke.

In these verses, the psalmist descends into deep despair. In this whole chapter, the writer has continually talked about his oppressors and his feelings have all been focused on the external. Here in these verses, it takes a turn and he focuses on his internal oppression. This oppression has taken him to a deep sense of despair.

The 11th Hebrew letter is **KAPH**. It also takes the notion that it means the outstretched hand, asking and weak. It brings us the idea that it encompasses anything that is hollow or outstretched in order to receive something.

Vs. 81-My
        SOUL faints and longs for Your
        SALVATION. I am
        WAITING with hope for Your
        WORD.

Vs. 82-My eyes grow heavy while I
        WATCH for your promises, I am
        WATING for comfort.

Vs. 83-There is
　　　　SMOKE in my eyes, I am
　　　　STEADILY focused on Your Word.

Vs. 84-How long do I have to
　　　　WAIT?
　　　　WHEN are you going to
　　　　PUNISH my
　　　　PERSECUTORS?

Vs. 85-The arrogant are
　　　　DIGGING
　　　　DITCHES to
　　　　TRAP me, they do not
　　　　TRUST Your law.

Vs. 86-I trust in Your
　　　　COMMANDS but they harass me without
　　　　CAUSE. Help me!

Vs. 87-They almost wiped me
　　　　FROM the earth, I have not
　　　　FORSAKEN your law.

Vs. 88-With Your unfailing
　　　　LOVE, preserve my
　　　　LIFE, so I
　　　　MAY obey the words from Your
　　　　MOUTH.

DARK DAYS

The psalmist gives us a glimpse of who his oppressors are throughout the verses in Psalms 119. Some of these oppressors are powerful men, and some of them are ungodly people. The psalmist never gives us why there is tension between him and these oppressors, but if you read the writings of this psalm you will notice the tension might be because he is always standing steadfast on the Word of God.

The writer has gone into despair and describes it as one whose soul is fainting and his eyes are burning and heavy and watery, and he can't see because there is smoke in his eyes. Then the writer wants to know how long he has to wait before he sees his oppressors punished. He even goes to the point where he so deep in despair that he is almost taken from this earth. Through this prayer and through the crying of his heart, he still stands firm on the Word of God.

I am sure you have encountered dark days, I know that I have. Maybe yours have been darker than mine, maybe mine has been darker than yours, but whichever the case might be, we must keep our focus and stand firm on God's Word.

The psalmist had been plunged into despair and the dark days were upon him. He says that he feels like "a bottle in the smoke." He had been through the fire, and now the smell of smoke is on him, it's in his eyes.

A BOTTLE IN THE SMOKE

Fortunately, I have never had to deal with a house fire, and fortunately, we have never lost our belongings in a house fire. Maybe you have experienced the sadness and trauma of a house fire, I pray that you haven't and I pray you never will. For a moment let's stop and think about what the psalmist means when he writes "I have become like a bottle in the smoke".

A few pages earlier I mentioned that I would stand by the fire and throw a bottle into the flames, and the next day I would check the bottle out. Here is what I learned from those times of throwing some old jars or bottles into the fire.

IT'S BEEN THROUGH THE FIRE-After the bottle had spent time in the fire we see what has happened. The bottle has become black and sooty. The bottle has an oily feel to it, and the bottle is ruined. Many of us have been through the fire. Many of us have spent many days or months in the fire. The psalmist has been through the fire. We also know when people or loved ones have been through the fire. We notice how their walking pace has slowed down, we notice they don't stand up as straight, and their speech lacks enthusiasm, and their eyes are burning and often filled with tears.

IT BECOMES FRAGILE-When the embers of the flame had cooled, I would go out to the burnt spot and grab a stick and poke the bottles or the jars. Some of those bottles would break, or if I went to pick one up, it would crumble in my hands. These bottles had become fragile from the intense heat. The flames had lashed continually for hours upon the glass. Many times in life, the flames seem to keep lashing out at us and burning us and we become like a bottle in the smoke. Life is fragile already, but when you go through the fire, it becomes, even more, fragile. After coming through the fire our energy is used up, the flames have taken their toll on our bodies, minds, and our spirits. We feel weak, we feel fragile, and sometimes we think we are going to break even at the lightest touch.

IT HAS BECOME FOREVER WORTHLESS- Those bottles that I retrieved from the flames would not make a good centerpiece for the dining room table. I would not put them on display on the mantle above the fireplace. I wouldn't take the jars and put them in the cabinet for my mother to use. I wouldn't refill the bottles and drink from them again. Many times people who have been in the fire are so burnt that they never return to who they used to be. Many times those people lose their potential for doing good. Some will never trust God again.

I hope and pray that you do not have any dark days. I hope and pray that you never have to go through the fire. I pray that you never have to experience deep despair in your life. But if you do, if I do may we remind ourselves of this passage and remember what the psalmist says "I have not forsaken Your Word".

HELP ME

The psalmist at one point in these few verses even cries out for help. He knows that he has not forsaken God or His Word, and yet his oppressors are still hot on his trail and they are trying to trip him up and throw him in a ditch. So he yells, "HELP ME!!"

We have been walking around in the darkest of days. We have been burnt by the flames and we have smoke in our eyes, they burn, they water, and the smell is still on us. We are afraid that we are going to be trapped and thrown into a ditch. Now, what do we do? We are crying for help, and raise our voices to the heavens. How do we overcome the darkness? How do we overcome the fire? The psalmist shows us what to do in these eight verses.

PATIENTLY WAITING-The psalmist states that he is "waiting on the Word of God." We must do the same. One thing we have continually seen throughout this psalm is that the writer keeps his hope in the Word of God. When the flames of life leap up to burn us we must watch for comfort because God will give it to us. When the darkness tries to overtake us, we must wait on God's Word. In the book of John, we are promised a comforter, the Holy Spirit, and he will come and bring us comfort. In the book of Isaiah we are told to "wait on the Lord" because when we learn to wait, we will be renewed. So what does it mean to "wait on the Lord"? How do we "wait on the Word"?

Most people would like to believe they are very patient when it comes to waiting. Maybe you are or maybe you are like me, impatient. When you go to the doctor or you go to the hospital they always have a room known as the "waiting" room. I am not real comfortable in that room because I, well, I have to WAIT. Maybe there are times when you get stuck in traffic depending on where you live. You are waiting to move an inch or two and it seems like hours have gone by as you move just a few feet. There are other kinds of waiting. Waiting for the right job, waiting for the right spouse, waiting on your house to sell so you can buy the one you want. Waiting in the long line at the grocery store, waiting for your kids to come home from school, or waiting for the time to clock out from your job and go home.

G. Campbell Morgan was a British Evangelist, preacher, and a leading Bible scholar. This is what he has to say about "waiting on the Lord"!

"Waiting for God is not laziness. Waiting for God is not going to sleep. Waiting for God is not the abandonment of effort. Waiting for God means first activity under command; second, readiness for any new command that may come; third, the ability to do nothing until the command is given.

The Hebrew word translated "waiting" . . . has an affinity with a word that means "to entrench." God works for him that entrenches himself in Him. The idea of waiting for God here is that of digging ourselves into God.

Waiting for God, then, means the power to do nothing save under command. This is not lack of power to do anything. Waiting for God needs strength rather than weakness. It is the power to do nothing. It is the strength that holds strength in check. It is the strength that prevents the blundering activity which is entirely false and will make the true activity impossible when the definite command comes.

Waiting is far more difficult than working. . . .
Waiting requires strength. It demands the
absolute surrender of the life to God, the
confession that we are at the end of our own
understanding of things, the confession that we
really do not see our way and do not know the
way. The waiting that says: "Until God shall speak
we dare not move and will not move, we will not
be seduced from our resolution to wait"; requires
strength. 34

PATIENTLY WATCHING-The psalmist says
that he will keep a "steady gaze" or watch on the
instructions from God. Even though his eyes are
getting heavy looking for a sign, and even though
his eyes are red, burning, itchy, and watery
because he has been standing in the fire, he
knows that he must watch for God's Word. We
must keep our eyes on the Word and in the Word.
We must always look to God in those dark days,
always watching for God. Corrie Ten Boom was a
survivor of the Holocaust. She once said, "Look
without and be distressed. Look within and be
depressed. Look at Jesus and be at rest." She had
every reason to be distressed and to look at the
things happening to her and around her. She had

every reason to look without. She lived in a concentration camp. She saw her sister and father—and many others—die at the hands of the Nazis. When she looked within, she felt depressed as she saw the darkness of her own heart. But seeing the example of her godly sister Betsy, who saw the bright side of everything and was always trusting God, she concluded, "Look at Jesus and be at rest."[35]

PATIENTLY WALKING-The psalmist says that the oppressors have tried to trip him up, tried to throw him in a ditch, but he hasn't "relaxed his grip" on the Word of God. He is still walking with God he is still walking in the Word. Many times Christians read the Word of God because they believe it is something that they have to do. We should want to do it, we should want to stroll through the pages and take our time as we read. There is nothing wrong with having a scheduled Bible reading where you read the Word in six months or a year, but I believe we just read to be reading. When we patiently walk we should take our time, look beyond the obvious. We should just walk, not run, not scan, not pop in and out, but slowly walk and enjoy the words that we are reading. When we take our time and walk through the pages we will find Him there.

SONG FROM THE HEART

The psalmist song of despair is reflected in verses 82-83 when he talks of his eyes failing, and he has become like "a bottle in the smoke." We have covered it quite extensively above in the previous pages, but we all face those days of fire, smoke and darkness. There is an old saying that has been used many times "Night is always darkest before the dawn". This phrase was actually coined by Thomas Fuller who was an English theologian and historian. His actual statement was this "It is always darkest just before the day dawneth." [36] Scientifically, this statement would not be true because it is darkest at midnight when the sun is on the opposite side of the earth. When this statement is made though it is not referring to science but rather circumstances we might be in at the time.

The psalmist believed that he was at one of the worst times of his life, being oppressed from the outside and at times from the inside. As we will see in the next chapter, the writer of this psalm surrenders himself to praise and worship and he knows the dawn is coming.

Johann Sebastian Bach was born into the musical family. At age 9 his mother had passed away and 9 months later he lost his father. He lived with an older brother, and at an early age, he had a burning desire to write music. At age 17, Bach became the organist at the church and not long after was in charge of the entire music ministry. Some at the church didn't like some of the music he composed and they complained that it was a little showy. In his defense for his writing, he said, "The main purpose of my music is to glorify God. Some people do this with music that is simple. I haven't chosen to use a simple style, but my music comes from my heart as a humble offering to God. This honors God no matter what musical style I use." He and the church could not agree, so he began to look for another job. One of the jobs he held was in Weimar, Germany where he wrote a new cantata every month. During one three-year period, he wrote, conducted, orchestrated, and performed with the choir and orchestra a new cantata every week. Bach left a legacy that still lives on today in this present world. At the beginning of every authentic manuscript, you will find the letters "J.J." which stands for Jesu Java (Jesus help me.). At the end of each original manuscript, you will find the letters "S.D.G." which stands for Soli Deo Gloria (to the glory of God).[37]

In the darkest hours and the hottest flames of Bach's life he turned to God and found a way to glorify God, he wrote music.

OUR PRAYER

Heavenly Father, when we face the dark days, and when we face the flames of life and our eyes are burning, red, and itchy help us keep our focus on you by waiting, watching, and walking in Your Word. In Jesus Name, Amen.

Song #12

"You Are Faithful"

"Through the clouds of midnight, this bright promise shone: 'I will never leave thee, never leave thee alone.'"[38]
Anonymous

Psalms 119:89-96

[89] *"Forever, O LORD, thy word is settled in heaven.*

[90] *Thy faithfulness is unto all generations: thou hast established the earth, and it abideth.*

[91] *They continue this day according to thine ordinances: for all are thy servants.*

[92] *Unless thy law had been my delights, I should then have perished in mine affliction.*

[93] *I will never forget thy precepts: for with them thou hast quickened me.*

[94] *I am thine, save me: for I have sought thy precepts.*

[95] *The wicked have waited for me to destroy me: but I will consider thy testimonies.*

189

⁹⁶ I have seen an end of all perfection: but thy commandment is exceeding broad."

The psalmist had just endured some of the darkest days of his life and had walked through the hottest flames, but yet he still knew that the Word of God is eternal and it stands firm. He has not totally escaped the clutches of darkness, but he lifts his voice in praise and adoration to God and His Word. He tells us in the verses above that God's Word is permanent, fixed, and that the truth of God is always up to date. He tells us that God is faithful.

The Hebrew letter that we see at the beginning of this section is **LAMED**. The verb *lamad* means to learn or teach. The derivative *talmid* means scholar and another derivative means ox goad. The letter *LAMED* is said to look like a goad and therefore, when Jesus said to Saul, "it is hard for you to kick against the goads" this was pointing more to learning than coercion.

Vs. 89-Your Word Lord is eternal and
        STAYS it
        STANDS firm in the heavens.

Vs. 90-You
        ARE faithful
        ALL the time, You have
        ESTABLISHED the
        EARTH and it
        ENDURES.

Vs. 91-Your Word is
        DEPENDABLE to this
        DAY and all things serve You.

Vs. 92-If I
        WOULD not have delighted in Your
        WORD, I
        WOULD have given up in the hard times.

Vs. 93-I will not forget Your
        PRECEPTS for with then You have
        PRESERVED my life.

Vs. 94-SAVE me, for I am all Yours, I have
        SOUGHT out Your Word.

Vs. 95-The
    WICKED are
    WAITING to destroy me, so I
    WILL think and ponder upon Your
    WORD.

Vs. 96-ALL things
    ARE limited but Your
    COMMANDS
    CAN'T be
    CONTAINED and are boundless.

FIRM

I would like to take a moment and talk about
God's Word and how it continues to stand firm,
how it is permanent like the heavens above.
Many have said or believed that the Word of God
is out of date and it does not apply to today.
Many have criticized the Word of God and
believing that the Word is not truth because men
wrote the words. The group, "Casting Crowns"
has a song titled "The Word is Alive" and in the
middle of this song they have a part where they
do not sing, they just talk and here is what they
say.

"The Bible was inscribed over a period of 2000
years
In times of war and in days of peace
By kings, physicians, tax collectors, farmers
Fishermen, singers, and shepherds

The marvel is that a library so perfectly cohesive
Could have been produced by such a diverse
crowd
Over a period of time which staggers the
imagination
Jesus is its grand subject, our good is designed
And the glory of God is its end" 39

In the book of Hebrews, God's Word is described
as being alive and active. It is described as being
sharper than any two-edged sword, and it can
penetrate the soul and the spirit, and it judges the
thoughts and attitudes of our hearts. Casting
Crowns in the song mentioned above describes
Hebrews 4:12 in the chorus.

"The word is alive
And it cuts like the sword through the darkness
With a message of life to the hopeless and the
frail

Breathing life into all who believe

The word is alive
And the world and its glories will fade
But its truth, it will not pass away
It remains yesterday and forever the same." 40

Since God's Word is eternal, faithful, and it is permanent then we must cherish the Word of God. We must read it, live it, use it and most of all love it. There are eight images the Word of God is compared to and I would like to take a quick look at these.

God's Word is like a Hammer

"Is not my word like fire," declares the LORD, "and like a hammer that breaks a rock in pieces" (Jeremiah 23:29 NIV)?

When you think about a hammer you think of two things, a hammer is used to break, and a hammer is used to build. The picture that God is painting with this verse is the Word of God functions like a sledgehammer, in which it is used to shatter and break down. Sometimes we build walls made of bricks and mortar that harden and hide our hearts

194

from God. There are times when we put up this stone wall and try to keep God out. Our sinful flesh thinks it can build up barriers, and we have a tendency to try to do things on our own. When we build these walls we put up a rock casing around our hearts and lives, and God knows we do this, so He uses His Word to break through, like a sledgehammer, smashing through the concrete and the stones. He uses the Word and the Holy Spirit to break through our stubborn hearts and rips out all that is rotten and replaces it with good.

 After the walls are broken he uses His word like a hammer to start the rebuilding process. Our hearts and lives are now "under construction" and the hammer is used to start putting boards and nails into place. The boards of hope are erected and the nails of forgiveness are hammered into place.

God's Word is like a Sword

"For the word of God is alive and active. Sharper than any double-edged sword, it penetrates even to dividing soul and spirit, joints and marrow; it judges the thoughts and attitudes of the heart" (Hebrews 4:12 NIV).

The first thing we see is the Word of God is a living, it is ALIVE. The Word of God is unlike any other book that you have in your home. The Library of Congress holds the claim of being the largest library in the world, with more than 150 million items on approximately 838 miles of bookshelves. The collections include more than 32 million books and other printed materials, 3.0 million recordings, 15 million photographs, 5 million maps, and 61 million manuscripts.

Yet among all these volumes there is only one that holds the claim of being alive and powerful and that is the Word of God. This claim places the Word of God in a unique category all on its own. The Word of God is continually at work.

A sharp sword can lay open the human body with one slashing blow, so the sword of the Word can open our inner life and expose it to ourselves and to others. There were two different type swords in the world of the Romans. There was a large sword it was long, heavy and destructive. There was a short sword called the machaira it was lightweight and double-edged and deadly because it cut both ways. The Word of God is sharper than the short double-edged sword and it will pierce our hearts and our souls, it will open up our thoughts and it will cut deep into our hearts revealing our attitudes.

God's Word is like a Fire

"Is not my word like fire," declares the LORD, "and like a hammer that breaks a rock in pieces" (Jeremiah 23:29 NIV)?

When we think of fire we usually think of a forest fire that is totally out of control or a house on fire that is consuming the whole house. We might even think of a fiery furnace which is used to heat up the glass, metal or used for a refining process. A small spark can start a blaze. When that blaze has been started and it is left alone it will consume everything in its path. When that fire starts to spread it will bring terror those who are living close by.

The Word is like that fire, it will consume. All of our hearts are subject to the flames of God. His Word aims to consume and expose our hearts. Any selfishness in our hearts will be consumed. Any pride we might have will be burned away.

Small sins, big sins any thought will be brought against the heat of God's Word.

God's Word also refines us, by revealing the truth. We are placed many times in the furnace of God and we have to stand in the flames, in the heat, and in the fire, and this is where the process of refining starts. There are some steps taken in the purification or refining process. The hardened ore is broken into pieces so that the gold and silver could be exposed to heat. Sometimes our hardened hearts need to be broken into pieces so that the gold and silver will be exposed. The broken pieces of ore are placed into the furnace of fire. Our broken hearts are placed into the furnace. Then as the heat and the fire start to melt those broken pieces the impurities will rise to the surface and they are skimmed off the top. When our lives are in the heat and the fire starts to melt our broken hearts the impurities of our hearts will rise to the surface so they can be taken away. The purification process has begun, and the refiner will skim the top and pull off the impurities and he sees a dim image of himself and so he turns up the heat for he knows at certain degrees, certain impurities will rise. Sometimes we are placed in the fire, and the fire has to be hotter so that all of our impurities will be skimmed off the top. The more impurities that are removed, the refiner can see his image in the gold or silver more clearly. When he can see his reflection clearly, then the process is done. When we are placed in the furnace and when we can see the image of Christ in our hearts then we know the process is done. In the book of Job, he says, "that when he is tested, he will come forth as gold."

God's Word is like a Light

"Your word is a lamp for my feet,
*   a light on my path" (Psalms 119:105 NIV).*

I find this verse very interesting because he uses the word "lamp" and then he uses the word "light". If you have ever been hiking at night or have gone camping at night, you find that it is very difficult to see anything in the dark. If you have a flashlight it is sufficient for the job of lighting your way, but it doesn't shine very far down the pathway, but we are able to see our next step.

God's Word is that flashlight, that lamp that shows us where our feet should go. One step at a time, the lamp will guide us. If you have a lamp or a lantern and you are on a dark pathway or trail at night, the lantern or light helps us see only one step ahead. When you take the next step the lantern or lamp moves forward and another step is made eventually leading you safely to your destination. The pathway has been lit, but only one step at a time. God uses His Word in the same manner guiding us one step at a time. Sometimes in life, the dark of the unknown can cast a veil over our pathways. Potential pitfalls, lurking dangers, and tragic missteps often cause the traveler to miss his steps and it will rob him of his peace, and confidence in which the Lord intended for him to enjoy.

When we stop worrying about tomorrow and start to trust God for today, we will find by the light of God's Word the grace and guidance we need in every situation. The Word of God provides light on our pathway. It isn't always necessary to see beyond what the Lord reveals. When we follow Him, there is always enough light for each step of the way.

God's Word is like a Honeycomb

"They are more precious than gold,
  than much pure gold;
they are sweeter than honey,
  than honey from the honeycomb" (Psalms
19:10 NIV).

Honey is a natural food and it is made by bees and eaten by humans. It has natural sugar and doesn't need to be refined. It doesn't need any chemical change or any additives. It is the world's perfect, natural sweetener. Honey is a natural food that has water, nutrients, vitamins minerals, acids, and sugar in the exact amounts. There is no substitute for honey and it is not man-made, and there is not an imitation product of honey. Honey is good for your body.

When you look at the verse above you see that God's Word is infinitely sweet. Just as honey is good for the body, the Word of God is good for life, it nourishes and strengthens us.

When we take in the Word of God we find there is no imitation Word, there is no substitute for feeding on the Word. We should enjoy the Word, and taste the sweetness of His Word. We taste the sweetness when we read it, meditate on it, and memorize it. We taste the sweetness when we believe it and obey it.

How does the Word of God taste to you? When we are physically sick we often find that food is distasteful, and when we become spiritually sick we lose the sweet taste of God's Word.

When we give out the Word of God we should taste how sweet it really is. To share the Word of God with our neighbors, our children, our grandchildren or our spouse, we find how sweet the Word is. It is sweet to testify with the words of Scripture and offer salvation and hope to a lost soul.

God's Word is like Medicine

"My son, pay attention to what I say;
 turn your ear to my words.
Do not let them out of your sight,
 keep them within your heart;
for they are life to those who find them
 and health to one's whole body.
Above all else, guard your heart,
 for everything you do flows from it" (Proverbs 4:20-23 NIV).

When you are physically ill and not feeling well, you make an appointment with the doctor and after the visit, he will usually prescribe some kind of medicine to take for a certain number of days. You go to the drug store and you purchase the prescription and you take it home and hopefully you take the medicine and start feeling better. I said "hopefully" because if you are like me, then you will start to feel better and you stop taking the medicine. They always tell you to "finish" the prescription.

God's Word is medicine for our souls, for our emotions, for our hearts, for our families, for our finances, for our stress, and even for our marriage.

Like medicine, God's Word must be taken to be effective. It doesn't work if it is sitting on the counter in the kitchen.

Like medicine, it has to be taken according to the directions. If you follow God's Word and His directions like you follow the doctor's orders, then you will see some great results and healing.

With any medicine, you have to be careful to not overdose by taking too much at one time. You can't however, overdose on God's Word. The more of His Word the better you are.

You have to purchase medicine when you go to the store to pick up your prescription. You do not have to purchase the Word of God; it is given to you for free.

With any medicine, if you are not feeling well soon, you have to keep taking the medicine you do not double up on the dosage. In your spiritual life, if you do not see results of getting better, you CAN double the dosage because more of His Word will not hurt you.

God's Word is like a Seed

"This is the meaning of the parable: The seed is the word of God" (Luke 8:11 NIV).

In Luke 8 a crowd had gathered and Jesus told them a parable about a farmer who had some seed and the farmer went out to scatter the seed. While he was scattering the seed, some fell on the path and the birds came and ate it, then some fell on the hard, stony ground, the plants withered because there was no moisture. Some of the seed fell among the thorns, which grew up and choked the plants. Some fell on good soil and grew up and yielded a crop. Jesus tells His disciples that the seed is the Word of God. He also says, "that whoever has ears to hear, let him hear. "

How do we respond to the Word of God?

Sometimes life is hard and sometimes it is unfair and sometimes we can respond to life with a hard heart. People will attack you, abuse you, gossip about you, slander you, and even hurt you. The Word of God is scattered into our lives but our heart response falls under the first condition where the seed just falls on the path and the birds come and eat it up. When we are hurt by others we get bitter and angry, and jealous and the devil comes along and snatches the Word right out of our hearts. We put up walls and block others and God's Word out.

Then the Word is scattered around on the hard, rocky ground. The Word comes to the person but it does not have a lasting impact for there is no moisture for the roots. The roots do not go deep into the heart. Sometimes this is when we or others go to church looking for that emotional lift. We hear the Word of God and we accept it with joy, but we don't do anything more with it when we leave the church building. There are times when people are struggling with some situations in their lives and they complain that their faith seems dry. They believe the church is no longer meeting their needs and they feel useless and empty. When you ask these people "Are you reading the Word of God?" They don't answer with a positive "yes". We go to church on Sunday mornings and want to be fed, but the rest of the week we feed off of the world. You are uplifted for a while because God's Word is good every time you hear it, but you can't live and stay uplifted if your roots do not have any moisture.

Next, the Word of God is scattered among the thorns of the heart. We hear the Word of God but when we start traveling on our way we become distracted and anxious. Instead of having our hearts and minds devoted to God, we are distracted with other things. When troubles come our way and we start trying to fix it with the world's wisdom and our own personal ambitions, then our hearts are full of thorns and we allow God's Word to be choked out.

Lastly, the Word of God is scattered on the good soil. These are the ones, who have a noble and good heart, and they hear the Word, and they retain it to persevere and they have a bountiful crop. When we have a good heart, and we hear the Word and we apply the Word in our life, then we will have a harvest of spiritual fruit. Every time the Word of God comes to you, whether you read it, hear it in church, hear it on the radio or the TV, any time the Word reaches your heart it is the condition of your heart which will dictate how you respond to the Word. A seed contains life; the Word of God contains life. We are awakened as we feast on God's Word. The image of Christ becomes clearer when we allow God's Word to grow inside us.

God's Word is like a Mirror

"Anyone who listens to the word but does not do what it says is like someone who looks at his face in a mirror and, after looking at himself, goes away and immediately forgets what he looks like. But whoever looks intently into the perfect law that gives freedom, and

continues in it—not forgetting what they have heard, but doing it—they will be blessed in what they do" (James 1:23-25 NIV).

Everyone has their morning routine. You might be one who gets up in the morning and you have to have that cup of coffee, or you might be the one who has to have a shower to wake up. Whatever your routine consists of, you probably have to look in the mirror at some point. You actually might have to look in the mirror more than once to make sure everything is looking good before you head out the door.

We also have a spiritual mirror. When we step out onto the porch we know that we have looked in the mirror to make sure our physical appearance is ready for the world to see. Have you stopped and thought about looking in the spiritual mirror before you leave your house?

When we see God's Word as a mirror, it will change how we view God's Word.

First, we will stop reading God's Word and thinking "Oh, so-and-so needs to hear that." When we read God's Word and think that it should apply to someone else, then we are looking into a mirror and hoping to see someone else's reflection. When we look into God's Word we see our own reflection, for this is how God has designed His Word.

Second, we will stop reading God's Word with the thought, "yawn...I've read this before." The mirror is unchanging, but every time we look in the mirror we get a different reflection of ourselves. God's Word is unchanging, but it still reflects back to us something different depending on our spiritual need.

Third, when we read something in God's Word, we do something about what we read. When we look into the mirror and we find a hair out of place, we do something about it. When we look into the mirror and we notice something needs to be changed, we do something about it. When we look into God's Word, we shouldn't just ignore what we read; we need to do something about it. We need to become doers of the Word. If we are not doing something about what we see in the mirror of God's Word, then we are fooling ourselves.

FAITHFULNESS

The psalmist writes and sings about the faithfulness of God when he expresses "Your faithfulness continues through all generations." Even though he had just had some dark days and he has been walking in the flames, he still knew God is faithful. The psalmist had been disappointed in his life many times and could have said "never expect anything from God." He didn't say that he continued to praise God and lift up the name of God because he knows that God is faithful.

Let's take some time over the next few pages and look at the faithfulness of God. In order not to write a whole other book, I will try to keep this brief and encourage you to study on your own the faithfulness of God.

GOD IS FAITHFUL BECAUSE OF HIS NAME

God is called God. God is called, "the faithful God". His faithfulness is unlimited, unfailing and abounding.

"Your love, LORD, reaches to the heavens, your faithfulness to the skies" (Psalms 36:5 NIV).

"Nevertheless my lovingkindness will I not utterly take from him, nor suffer my faithfulness to fail" (Psalms 89:33 KJV).

"Because of the LORD's great love we are not consumed, for his compassions never fail. They are new every morning; great is your faithfulness" (Lamentations 3:22-23 NIV).

GOD IS FAITHFUL BECAUSE OF HIS NATURE

He is called, "the faithful God". When you look at the word faithful, it speaks of one who supports, and confirms. It speaks of one who can be believed. Simply stated, God is one in whom we can put complete trust.

Friends will fail, the family will fail, our funds will fail, our feelings will fail, and our faith will fail, but God is faithful.

In every realm of life, God is faithful to stand by His promises. He will save you, help you, hear you, meet your needs, give you grace, give you peace, and walk with you every step of the way.

"If you declare with your mouth, "Jesus is Lord," and believe in your heart that God raised him from the dead, you will be saved. For it is with your heart that you believe and are justified, and it is with your mouth that you profess your faith and are saved" (Romans 10:9-10 NIV).

"Call to me and I will answer you and tell you great and unsearchable things you do not know" (Jeremiah 33:3 NIV).

"And my God will meet all your needs according to the riches of his glory in Christ Jesus" (Philippians 4:19 NIV).

"But he said to me, "My grace is sufficient for you, for my power is made perfect in weakness." Therefore I will boast all the more gladly about my weaknesses, so that Christ's power may rest on me" (2 Corinthians 12:9 NIV).

"Do not be anxious about anything, but in every situation, by prayer and petition, with thanksgiving, present your requests to God. And the peace of God, which transcends all understanding, will guard your hearts and your minds in Christ Jesus" (Philippians 4:6-7 NIV).

"Keep your lives free from the love of money and be content with what you have, because God has said, 'Never will I leave you; never will I forsake you" (Hebrews 13:5 NIV).

There is so much more we can talk about when it comes to the faithfulness of God, but for time and space purposes, I would ask that you take the time to look into the Word of God and search out His faithfulness.

SONG FROM THE HEART

Crushed and defeated, and the darkness overtaking him, but yet the writer knew that God was his strength and the Word of God is what He could rely on. The psalmist even said that he could see boundaries or limits to everything that deals with humanity, but God's Word has no boundaries and it is "firmly fixed" in the heavens. He expressed it in verse 89 when he says "Your Word stands firm in the heavens."

One of the most dramatic examples of the Scriptures divine ability to transform men and women involved the famous mutiny on the Bounty. Following their rebellion against the notorious Captain Bligh, nine mutineers, along with the Tahitian men and women, found their way to Pitcairn Island, a tiny dot in the South Pacific only two miles long and a mile wide. Ten years later, drink and fighting had left only one man alive, John Adams. Eleven women and 23 children made up the rest of the Island's population.

About this time, Adams came across the Bounty's Bible in the bottom of an old chest. He began to read it, and the divine power of God's Word.... reached into the heart of that hardened man on a tiny volcanic speck in the vast Pacific Ocean.... and changed his life forever.
The peace and love that Adams found in the Scriptures entirely replaced the old life of quarreling, brawling, and liquor.

He began to teach the children from the Bible until every person on the island had experienced the same amazing change that he had found. 41

No heart is too tough and no soul is too dark.
 When God wills it, his word can pierce anyone as a certain Mr. Thorpe in the 18th century Bristol found out.
Thorpe was a part of a band of men who called themselves, the "Hell Fire Club." Their reason for existence was to mock and ridicule the work of the famed evangelist, George Whitefield. On one occasion, the "Hell-Fire Club" gathered at a pub for such mockery. Mr. Thorpe offered his brilliant imitation of Whitefield, whom he and his friends called, "Mr. Squintum" because of Whitefield's

eyes. Thorpe delivered his mocking sermon with brilliant accuracy, perfectly imitating Whitefield's tone and facial expressions as he quoted Scripture.

Suddenly amidst the laughter, Thorpe had to sit down for he was pierced through and was converted on the spot.

Mr. Thorpe was a thoroughly nasty man, engaged in nasty actions yet the Word of God pierced his heart and changed him and in an instant. Mr. Thorpe went on to be a prominent Christian leader in the city of Bristol. [42]

OUR PRAYER

Heavenly Father, when I am down, crushed and hurting help me remember Your Word is firm, and You are faithful. When I am ready to give up, help me to rely on Your strength because you will strengthen me. In Jesus Name, Amen.

Song #13

"Sweeter Than Honey"

"Continue to connect with God through His Word, relish every morsel. After all, His words are sweeter than honey!"[43]
Joe Stowell

Psalms 119:97-104

[97] *O how love I thy law! It is my meditation all the day.*

[98] *Thou through thy commandments hast made me wiser than mine enemies: for they are ever with me.*

[99] *I have more understanding than all my teachers: for thy testimonies are my meditation.*

[100] *I understand more than the ancients, because I keep thy precepts.*

[101] *I have refrained my feet from every evil way, that I might keep thy word.*

[102] *I have not departed from thy judgments: for thou hast taught me.*

[103] *How sweet are thy words unto my taste! Yea, sweeter than honey to my mouth!*

104 Through thy precepts I get understanding: therefore I hate every false way."

In the last chapter, we discussed some images that are used in the Bible to describe God's Word. One of those images dealt with verse 103 mentioned in this section. When I was younger and even today, there are a lot of foods that I do not like. Honestly, vegetables were never my favorite thing to eat, and some of them are still not today. I remember my parents would always beg me to eat my vegetables because they were "good for me". There were probably some other things that were put on the table that didn't look very appetizing, and didn't taste good either, and there was a lot of coaxing, begging, and even a few threats thrown my direction to try and get me to eat what was in front of me. One thing I have always enjoyed and that was the taste of honey.

I used to put honey on bread and eat it. It didn't take any begging whatsoever to get me to eat it. The psalmist describes God's Word as sweet even sweeter than honey. Now, in all honesty, I don't know if we can share the same sentiments as the writer of this psalm. Can you and I really say that we enjoy God's Word so much that it is sweet to us, sweeter than honey? Most of us, if not all of us, would probably be more apt to say "Well, I guess it is good for me, so I guess I will read it." When we go into reading the Word of God with that attitude, then we will walk away believing that God's Word is bland, and carries no flavor.

The 13th Hebrew letter is **MEM**. It carries with it the idea of a large body of water like a sea or an ocean. It is suggested that the letter looks like a wave.

Vs. 97-Oh, how I
　　　　LOVE your
　　　　LAW. I meditate on it all day
　　　　LONG.

Vs. 98-Your
　　　　WORD is always
　　　　WITH me, never obsolete. It makes me
　　　　WISER than my enemies.

Vs. 99-I have
　　　　MORE insight than
　　　　MY teachers. I always
　　　　MEDITATE on Your Word.

Vs. 100-I am
   WISER than the
   WISE ones of old. I simply do
   WHAT you tell me to do.

Vs. 101-I am careful where I walk,
   AVOIDING ditches and evil paths, spending
   ALL my time in Your Word.

Vs. 102-I do not
   DEPART or make
   DETOURS from Your Word. You
   DIRECT me, and teach me.

Vs. 103-Your Word is
   SWEET to
   MY taste, they are
   SWEETER than honey to
   MY
   MOUTH.

Vs. 104-I gain understanding from Your
   WORD, I hate every
   WRONG path.

BECOMING A STUDENT

If you are a Christian and you have read the entire
Bible all the way from Genesis through Revelation,

then you are in a very small minority in today's world. Many Christians are illiterate when it comes to the Bible. Many Christians have no knowledge of the Bible.

In order to be a student of anything, you have to study that subject. If you want to be a student of philosophy then you have to study philosophy. If you want to be a student of movie trivia then you have to study movies. If you want to be a student of God then you must study God's Word.

The psalmist stated that he "meditated" or studied the Word of God all day long. We might not be able to study the Word all day, but I am sure we can study it more than we do. Let's take the time and explore why Christians do not become students of the Word of God.

WE SEE THE BIBLE AS JUST ANOTHER BOOK

Some people think that because they have read the Bible, then they are good. They do not see the importance in keeping on reading. Some think the Bible is just full of stories and it has no real meaning or application. These people will become nothing more than the occasional Bible reader.

WE HAVE SOME FEAR OF NOT UNDERSTANDING

There are a lot of people who are afraid because they don't think they can understand what they are reading. The problem with this line of thinking will result in two thoughts. First, you will never be able to understand something if you don't seek to understand. Second, this is really more of an excuse to not study than it is a reason why we don't study. We have to learn to ask questions about what we don't understand. Ask someone who is more knowledgeable of the Bible. There is no one person who understands everything that is in the Bible, but we study and learn more as we grow in Christ.

WE FAIL TO SEE THE IMPORTANCE OF STUDYING

Sometimes we or others do not see it as a necessity to study but more of an option. Because we see it as an option, then we usually opt out of studying and make excuses of why we don't. It is natural that if you do not see something as a priority or an importance then you are not going to do it. We must grasp the importance of the study of God's Word.

WE ARE SIMPLY COMPLACENT AND APATHETIC

Most people who attend a church that are not really students of the Word fit into this category more than the others we have mentioned. I believe most of it is because we become lazy and uncaring. I believe that we have a tendency not to study because we do not care to study and we will always say that we do not have time.

Now let's take a few moments and explore reasons on why we should become students of the Word of God.

SOLID AND SOUND TEACHING

God's Word is a necessity and will lead us to sound teaching and truth. You cannot find real truth apart from God's Word you cannot find real direction apart from God's Word. Throughout history, there have been many who have littered the highway with their misinterpretations of scripture, and they have inaccurately taught the Word. There have been many people who have twisted the Word of God in order to justify their own actions and opinions. They have also twisted the doctrines to make them fit their own ideas so they can appear right. There are others who take their beliefs and try to make the Bible fit their beliefs.

It has always been my goal and hope that you don't take what you read, or listen to and blindly accept the teaching because the person writing or speaking holds a position, a title, or a following. Every time I have preached I urge people to go home and search out what I say and compare it to the Word of God. If you are reading this book, I would ask the same thing. When you read this book, and you have a question on something I have written, then search it out and compare it to the Word of God. We need to be such a diligent student of the Word that we can tell a difference between the fake and false teachers and the truth.

STANDING STRONG

We must become students of the Word of God so we can stand strong against temptations.

We have to be able to distinguish the difference between right and wrong. We are able to do this when we study the Word of God because it is God's standard and it teaches us right from wrong. The psalmist talked earlier about standing strong against temptation when he tells us to "hide the Word in our hearts so that we will not sin against God." In order to take this stand, you must study and feast on the Word, which is your source of strength.

We must become students of the Word of God so we can stand strong against problems. There are so many problems that we face today, and a lot of those problems would be avoided if we would seek the Word of God. You know how many problems we could avoid and be spared from if we would follow God's commands and God's principles that are outlined in His Word? We can be saved from so many mistakes, heartaches, relationship troubles, financial problems and difficult times if we would become more of a student and follower of God and His Word than a student and follower of our own thinking. Not all problems in life can be avoided, but I believe we can avoid quite a few if we would know what God says in His Word.

STEADILY GROWING FAITH

The reason people die spiritually is because they lack nourishment and that nourishment comes from the Word of God. There are some preachers in the world today who have quit preaching the truth and they refuse to preach anything with real sustenance. The result of that kind of preaching will draw big numbers, but there is no spiritual depth at all. Have you ever been invited to dinner and when you get there you were expecting a good dinner, therefore you show up hungry, and when you get there all they have are finger foods. This has happened to me, and I have found myself stopping somewhere on the way home to get a meal. Many times this is what happens in church. We go to church expecting a good meal, but we are only are fed finger foods and we leave the church service hungry and miserable. The Word of God is necessary for our own spiritual growth.

We must become a student of God's Word, so we must find a regular time and a regular place to do this. Humans are creatures of habit, so if we make it a habit of studying and reading God's Word, we will continue to do so. We must find a private place that is free from distractions. Turn off the TV, and find a quiet room away from people. Schedule a time and make that God's time. We also must find ways that will help us study and help us learn. Write down questions that you have, underline things, and highlight words or sentences. You might do it different than someone else, but it is important to learn how to study the Word and find out what works best for you.

The psalmist writes in verses 99-100 that he has become smarter than his teachers and wiser than the wise elders. When you become a regular, consistent student of the Word of God, then you can make the bold claim as the psalmist did. You will become wiser than those who oppose you with ungodly actions. You will become smarter than the worldly teachers. You will have more understanding more than those who have lived long and lived according to the world.

HOW SWEET IT IS

We have touched on this subject in the last chapter and at the beginning of this chapter. I am an avid chocolate eater. I love chocolate. It can come in the form of cookies, cake, ice cream, donuts, or candy. I have always said that "Chocolate is a gift from God." There are times when I crave chocolate. Maybe you crave it as well. In verse 103 it says *"How sweet are your words to my taste, sweeter than honey to my mouth!"*

Out of all the things the Israelites ate in the Old Testament, honey was one of the delicacies the Israelites enjoyed. I would relate this verse as the Word of God being "sweet to my taste, sweeter than chocolate". One of the things I enjoy most as previously stated is chocolate. I just finished reading a book the other day called "Sweeter Than Chocolate" by Christy Bower. She writes the whole book designed to help us become "addicted" to God's Word, just as I am "addicted" to chocolate.

In the book, she mentions craving chocolate, and ask the question "Do we crave God's Word the way we crave chocolate?" She stresses the idea of gaining a healthy addiction to God's Word. She also tells us there are different approaches to studying God's Word, just as there are different approaches when we enter into the sweet indulgences of chocolate. Paraphrasing what Christy has said in her book, see if you can identify yourself in these approaches.

Some people are NIBBLERS. Some just want to graze on bits of food here and there. After a meal, maybe you are satisfied with a small amount of chocolate. Many have a tendency to treat God's Word the same way, we tend to graze and nibble on Bible verses here and there, being satisfied with a small amount of God's Word, never broadening our experience in the smorgasbord of God's Word.

Some people use the PINCH and SCRATCH METHOD. You have seen these people at Valentine's Day when they receive a box of chocolates. You know the ones, with the swirly designs on top. You look at all of them in the box, trying to remember which ones you liked, and which ones had the creamy center or the coconut.

After spending much time, looking over all of them you pick up a chocolate and pinch it or scratch it to reveal the contents inside to see if that is the one you want to eat. Many people take the same approach and method when it comes to God's Word. We are just as picky, we tend to pick and choose the parts of the Bible we like. Some have a tendency to dwell only on the New Testament while others want to dwell only on the Old Testament. When we do this, we scratch the surface of God's Word, we have to dig deeper to taste the smorgasbord of delighting in the Word.

There are others that use the HOT FUDGE SUNDAY WITH A CHERRY ON TOP approach. One of our local ice cream stores is "Braum's", and every time we enter there I get the same thing. I am a creature of habit in a big, big way. When I order my ice cream I always get the "hot fudge Sunday." I always get the chocolate chip cookie dough ice cream, two scoops, and then hot fudge, with almonds and whip cream. I usually leave the cherry off of the top. Some people have a tendency to approach God's Word in the same manner. We want God's Word served up in a nice presentation and we never make any effort to experience God's Word for ourselves. When it comes to God's Word, we rather go to the ice cream store and get our treat, instead of bringing it home and eating it there.

I have never been to a chocolate buffet or a SMORGASBORD of chocolate. This is the way we should look at God's Word. The Word contains many flavors and varieties, in all sorts of presentations, and guess what, they are all good. When we look at God's Word we can never over-eat. It is calorie free and very nutritious. So dig in, eat it, chew it, and digest it. It is SWEETER than CHOCOLATE.

One more idea that I want to point out that Christy Bower talks about and that is the idea of convenience store chocolate compared to gourmet chocolate. I have never eaten much gourmet chocolate, usually, I grab the chocolate candy bars from the convenience store. Sometimes we treat God's Word in the same pattern; we rather just grab a candy bar from the shelf than indulge in gourmet chocolate. Look what Christy has to say. "Sometimes we settle for the convenience store version of God's Word. We want it easy, without much investment on our part. We look for grab-n-go verses or a pre-packaged daily devotional instead of taking the time to savor the richness of all God's Word has to offer.

The convenience store approach shapes our attitudes toward the Bible. We've become accustomed to grab-n-go convenience so if we have to slow down to understand something, we become frustrated and impatient. It's easier to blame the Biele for being difficult than to admit our impatience.

Yes, some parts of the Bible require us to slow down to gain a full understanding, but gourmet chocolate is meant to be savored, not gobbled up." [44]

SONG FROM THE HEART

 As we have previously stated, we see that verse 103 is the major song the psalmist is singing. *""How sweet are your words to my taste, sweeter than honey to my mouth!"*

So how do we become addicted to the Word of God? How do we crave the sweet taste of God's Word? I am a chocoholic, you could say I am addicted to chocolate. How did I become addicted? I tasted it, liked it, and wanted more. The more I ate it, then I wanted it even more. Look at what Christy Bower says, "Here's how I describe the steps to addiction:

1. Taste brings delight.
2. Delight creates desire.
3. Desire seeks opportunity.
4. Opportunity confirms delight.
5. Delight increases desire.
6. Repeat steps 3-5 until it is desired above all else." [45]

When you take the time to pause and think about the things you are addicted to, whether it is chocolate, shopping, shoes, clothes, or work, how does this play a part in your life regarding God's Word? Do we enjoy God's Word more than watching the TV? Do we enjoy it more than our computer? Do we enjoy it more than our phones? We need to develop a healthy addiction to God's Word, and this would probably include shutting off the TV, the computer, and putting away our phones.

Look what it says in the book of Ezekiel.

"Only take care, son of man, that you don't rebel like these rebels. Open your mouth and eat what I give you."

When I looked he had his hand stretched out to me, and in the hand a book, a scroll. He unrolled the scroll. On both sides, front and back, were written lamentations and mourning and doom.

He told me, "Son of man, eat what you see. Eat this book. Then go and speak to the family of Israel."

As I opened my mouth, he gave me the scroll to eat, saying, "Son of man, eat this book that I am giving you. Make a full meal of it!"

So I ate it. It tasted so good—just like honey" *(Ezekiel 2:8-3:3 MSG).*

God has handed His Word to you, open your mouth, eat it, make it a meal and enjoy it.

It has been said, "You are what you eat." We become what we read. When God's Word gets inside of us, it changes us from the inside out. Look at the following illustration.

"My mother-in-law hates mangoes. She's hated them for many years and with good reason. When she was a little girl, she was brought up on a dairy farm and since it made good sense to drink the milk they produced rather than buying it from the shop, they kept a house cow in a shed nest to the house and it provided milk for the family. Unfortunately, the property next door had a mango tree which hung over the fence and the mangoes dropped on the property. The cow loved to eat the mangoes, and the result, believe it or not, was mango-flavored milk all the time. So to this day, she can't stand mangoes. She was about 12 years old before she discovered that all milk wasn't mango flavored. Nobody knows it better than that cow that what you eat, flavors what you produce. This also applies to spiritual food-God's Word." [50]

OUR PRAYER

Heavenly Father, please give us Your wisdom, and help us taste Your Word, and become addicted to Your Word, may the words you give us be sweeter than honey and sweeter than chocolate. In Jesus Name, Amen.

Song #14

"Light My Way"

"Light gives of itself freely, filling all available space. It does not seek anything in return; it asks not whether you are friend of foe. It gives of itself and is not thereby diminished." [47]
Michael Strassfeld

Psalms 119:105-112

[105] *Thy word is a lamp unto my feet, and a light unto my path.*

[106] *I have sworn, and I will perform it, that I will keep thy righteous judgments.*

[107] *I am afflicted very much: quicken me, O LORD, according unto thy word.*

[108] *Accept, I beseech thee, the freewill offerings of my mouth, O LORD, and teach me thy judgments.*

[109] *My soul is continually in my hand: yet do I not forget thy law.*

[110] *The wicked have laid a snare for me: yet I erred not from thy precepts.*

¹¹¹ Thy testimonies have I taken as an heritage for ever: for they are the rejoicing of my heart.

¹¹² I have inclined mine heart to perform thy statutes alway, even unto the end."

A few chapters ago, we introduced eight things the Word of God is like and one of those things we mentioned was a light or a lamp. In verse 105, the psalmist tells us that God's Word is like a lamp for our feet and a light for our path. If you have ever walked out into the darkness in order to see you have to carry a light of some kind. In this day and age, we do not carry lamps like they did in the Bible days, today we have flashlights, and over the years they have made those stronger and the light can shine farther. We even have apps on our phone, or like my phone, the flashlight app is already installed. One thing we know about darkness and light is that light will always overcome the darkness, but darkness cannot overcome the light. In the book of John, it says, *"The light shines in the darkness, and the darkness has not overcome it."*

The 14th letter of the Hebrew alphabet is the letter **NUN**. The verb means to propagate or to increase. Derivative means offspring or posterity. The letter is often said to mean and resemble a fish, but the word *nun* is not used this way in the Bible. Instead, the word for fish comes from another verb which means multiply, or increase. The letter *nun* is written when it occurs at the end of a word, and when it occurs at the beginning or half-way a word.

Vs. 105-Your Word is a
      LAMP for my feet, and a
      LIGHT for my path.

Vs. 106-I have made a
      COMMITMENT and it has been
      CONFIRMED. I follow Your righteous laws.

Vs. 107-I have suffered much
      PAIN,
      PRESERVE my life with Your Word.

Vs. 108-Accept the praise from
      MY
      MOUTH and teach
      ME Your laws.

Vs. 109-I constantly take my
   LIFE in my hands, I will not forget Your
   LAWS.

Vs. 110-The wicked do
   THEIR best to
   THROW me off
   TRACK. I do not
   STRAY or
   SWERVE from Your Word.

Vs. 111-Your Word is my
   HERITAGE forever, they are the joy of my
   HEART.

Vs. 112-My
   HEART is
   SET on keeping Your Word, I always
   HAVE and I always will do what You
   SAY.

The psalmist in verse 105 says the Word is a "lamp for my feet" and a "light for my path." This verse is one of the most popular verses in the Bible. Amy Grant made this verse popular when she sang the song "Thy Word". Many books have been written with the words of verse 105 as the title. So why is this verse so special? Why is this verse so popular? It is because this verse has been stated so simply, but yet its meaning is so profound. God's Word is our light in a very dark world. God's Word is a beacon of light in the spiritual darkness and it shines a light on the path that shows us the way home. Sometimes we can get lost in life. We become distracted by all of the things around us, and we can feel like we have lost our place in this world. Even with good intentions, we can get lost in life because there are so many decisions we have to make. There is power in this verse because of the truth it tells of, but there is also power in this verse because we can apply this truth in our lives.

TURN ON YOUR HEADLIGHTS

We have mentioned part of this in an earlier chapter, but I would like to expound upon it some more in this chapter. The psalmist starts this section of verses out with this verse, speaking of God's Word as a lamp and a light.

Not too long ago, my son had driven to school which is south of where we live, not far, but far enough when your headlights all go out at once it can make for a difficult drive. One headlight had gone out earlier in the week, and we didn't have a chance to change it, and a few nights later he came home from school, because he had one evening class, and he told us that he had to drive home with no headlights and it was very hard to see. Needless to say, we went to the store and bought two lights and I replaced them that evening. Driving down the road with no headlights can be frightening, and nerve racking. Walking through the woods on a dark path can give you an eerie feeling. Yet, there are times in our Christian life when we don't turn on our headlights, or grab a flashlight. Sometimes we make decisions without consulting the Word of God or even praying, in other words, we don't turn on our headlights. Let's take a look at how important light is to us in our everyday lives.

First we will notice that LIGHT IS CRUCIAL. We need light to help us in our daily activities. I wouldn't be typing this book in the dark. At work, it would be very difficult to do what we have to do in the dark. The Word of God is a light, a lamp, and it is essential to our lives. We need it to make decisions.

Second we will notice that LIGHT CLARIFIES OUR WAY. When we are trying to read the small print on the back of a bottle, we will hold it under the light so we can read it better. Sometimes when we want to see things clearer, we will hold them under a light. God's Word is the light that clarifies our ways when we find ourselves walking around in the eerie darkness of life. When our days seem dark we need the light to help us navigate through the darkness.

Third we notice that LIGHT CARRIES US. When we are taking steps in the dark we can't see what is in front of us and we become unsure of our next step. Light will carry us on one step at a time. The light of God's Word will help us see our next step it will carry us through the darkness.

I'VE GOT JOY DOWN IN MY HEART

The psalmist states, "The Word of God is my heritage forever it is the joy of my heart." When we pick up the Word or read it off of our tablet, or read the scripture from our phone, do we enjoy it? Can we make the same proclamation as the psalmist? Over the last few chapters we have covered a lot of material ranging from God's Word being like a hammer, medicine, a light, a lamp, a honeycomb, and even sweeter than chocolate, and throughout all of those items can we boldly proclaim, "it is the joy of my heart"? I would essentially say that most of us could not make that statement. Most of us will start to read the Word and we get to a part we don't understand and we get tired of it or bored.

Some people find delight in reading books of all kind of genres or topics, but when it comes to reading the Bible we have a hard time with it.

As I am writing this book we are embarking upon leaving the old year and stepping into a new one in a little over one week. January 1 will roll around and many of us will attempt to make a resolution, but we will make a greater attempt to keeping that resolution. Some of us will make a resolution to go on a diet. We have thoughts such as "this year will be different, this year I will succeed." By the third week or maybe even earlier we have already given up on the chance of losing weight.

Christians sometimes face the same dilemma. January 1 rolls around and we make a resolution to read the entire Bible. By the third week, we have already found ourselves into the book of Leviticus or Numbers and we become discouraged and we never attempt to finish reading. There are precious treasures in the Word of God. It is like a deep mine filled with gold, silver and precious gems, but we must take the time to dig them out.

John Quincy Adams, sixth president of the United States, once said: "I speak as a man of the world to men of the world, and I say to you: "Search the Scriptures. The Word of God is our light. In it, we come to know God. In it, we come to know His will for us. Through it, we have the strength to stand against our enemies and endure persecution in this life. This is our eternal heritage. The book is open. It is before us. We must not miss out on what it contains." [48]

We have to learn that God's Word is not boring and to do that we have to learn how to read it, but not just read, learn how to apply it to our lives. When we learn how to apply what we read to our daily lives, then we find those treasures and we are not easily bored. Christy Bower in her book "Sweeter than Chocolate" gives some ideas of how we can make the Word of God not a boring thing but a joyful experience. Look at what she says about becoming addicted to the Word of God and loving it. I am going to use her words, but replace her name with mine, or you can put your name in the same spot as hers and mine.

"Hi, my name is Dale (insert your name here) and I am a chocoholic. I can't help it. I love chocolate. I love how it makes me feel. I think about it all the time. If I'm not eating chocolate, I'm dreaming about the next time I'll be able to enjoy it. I have an addiction to chocolate. Sounds plausible, doesn't it? Well, how about this next scenario? Does this next one sound like it could be you? Hi, my name is Dale (insert your name here) and I am a Bible-aholic. I can't help it. I love the Bible. I love how it makes me feel. I think about it all the time. If I'm not reading the Bible, I'm dreaming about the next time I'll be able to enjoy it. I have an addiction to the Bible. Does that one sound like you? Maybe not yet, but give it time and it could be." [49]

Enjoying the sweet taste of chocolate brings joy to my heart. Enjoying the sweet taste of God's Word should bring joy to my heart and yours.

SONG FROM THE HEART

As we have already seen the song the psalmist is singing is verse 105, and he proclaims it loud and clear, the Word of God is our light and we should be joyful because of it. We need to become a testimony to others showing them that the power of God's Word will illuminate darkened lives and transform them from being lost to being on a journey with God.

I found an article in a National Geographic magazine titled "Power of Light". I don't have space and time to share with you the whole article, but I found some interesting thoughts on the power of light.

"There has been light from the beginning. There will be light, feebly, at the end. In all its forms—visible and invisible—it saturates the universe. Light is more than a little bit inscrutable. Modern physics has sliced the stuff of nature into ever smaller and more exotic constituents, but light won't reduce. Light is light— pure, but not simple. No one is exactly sure how to describe it. A wave? A particle? Yes, the scientists

say. Both. It is a measure of light's importance in our daily lives that we hardly pay any attention to it. Light is almost like air. It's a given. A human would no more linger over the concept of light than a fish would ponder the notion of water.

There are exceptions, certain moments of sudden appreciation when a particular manifestation of light, a transitory glory, appears—a rainbow, a sunset, a pulse of heat lightning in a dark sky, the shimmering surface of the sea at twilight, the dappled light in a forest, and the little red dot from a professor's laser pointer. Stained glass in a church, backlit by a bright sky. The flicker of a candle, flooding a room with romance. The flashlight searching for the circuit breakers after a power outage.

The more you look at the topic, the more you realize that our lives are built around light, that our daily existence is continuously shaped—and made vivid— by that ambiguous stuff that dates from the beginning of time. From our technology to our spiritually, we are creatures of light." **50**

OUR PRAYER

Heavenly Father, may Your Word be our light and our guide. Help us to live by Your Word and help us to shine our light into the world. Help us to realize that the Word of God is our joy. In Jesus Name, Amen.

Song #15

"OH, I STAND IN AWE OF YOU"

"I am mentally preparing myself for the five-year-old mind. I want to come down to their physical limitations and up to their sense of wonder and awe." **51**
Shinichi Suzuki

Psalms 119:113-120

113 "I hate vain thoughts: but thy law do I love.

114 Thou art my hiding place and my shield: I hope in thy word.

115 Depart from me, ye evildoers: for I will keep the commandments of my God.

116 Uphold me according unto thy word, that I may live: and let me not be ashamed of my hope.

117 Hold thou me up, and I shall be safe: and I will have respect unto thy statutes continually.

118 Thou hast trodden down all them that err from thy statutes: for their deceit is falsehood.

248

119 Thou puttest away all the wicked of the earth like dross: therefore I love thy testimonies.

120 My flesh trembleth for fear of thee; and I am afraid of thy judgments."

When I read the above quote it drew my attention to the thought of how sometimes we should want to be like a child because many times they find wonder and awe in things that adults usually don't. Shinichi Suzuki worked with children and invented the Suzuki method of teaching music. When he taught children he came to understand that children had the ability to learn things well, especially in the right environment, and his goal was to develop the heart of the child and build character through music education. In the NIV version and other versions, the psalmist states at the end of this section that he "stands in awe" of God and His Word. The King James Version says "for fear of thee" which we understand as a "reverential fear" or being in awe.

The 15th letter of the Hebrew alphabet is **SAMEKH**. The verb *samak* means to lean upon, support or uphold. It is the verb that is used in the phrase "laying on of hands."

Vs. 113-Double-minded people I
     HATE, but I
     LOVE Your Word.

Vs. 114-You are my
     REFUGE, my shield and safe
     RETREAT. I have hope and I am
     RENEWED with Your Word.

Vs. 115-GET away evil doers, so I can keep
     GOD'S word.

Vs. 116-PRESERVE me according to Your
     PROMISE God, I will live.
     DO not let my hopes be
     DASHED.

Vs. 117-Uphold me, and I will be
     DELIVERED, I will always regard Your
     DECREES.

Vs. 118-Expose all those who
     DRIFT from Your
     DECREES. Their
     DELUSIONS are nothing.

Vs. 119-The wicked of earth You
    DISCARD like the
    DROSS. I
    EMBRACE
    EVERYTHING You say.

Vs. 120-I will
    STAND in awe of Your Word. I am
    SPEECHLESS with reverence.

PEER PRESSURE

At some point in your life, I am sure you have experienced some kind of peer pressure, the negative kind. We all have experienced the pressure to take unnecessary risks, tell lies, cheat, steal, or compromise our values and ethics. The psalmist had to deal with it just like we have had to deal with it. In verse 115, he wanted the evildoers to "get out of his life," so that he could live by God's Word. Peer pressure to compromise is strong, and in verse 116 he asks God to uphold him and sustain him so that he would not be put to shame.

Peer pressure is all around us from children to youth to adults. Everyone wants to feel accepted and they want to be loved. The natural desire of people is to have approval, to seek affection, and to seek out good will from our friends. We all have the desire to be accepted by family, friends, teachers, coaches, spouses, employers, and co-workers.

Definition

We have positive peer pressure and negative peer pressure. So what is peer pressure? It is defined as: "Social pressure by members of one's peer group to take a certain action, or adopt certain values, or conform in order to be accepted."

Discernment

Everyone is affected by peer pressure. We have to use discernment when it comes to pressure from our peers. I believe the youth of today have tremendous amounts of pressure and these include such things as violence, gangs, alcohol/drugs, sex, bad language, disrespect for parents, and friends. Adults also face pressure which included in the list are friends, drinking, cheating on their spouse, and immoral living. The Bible warns us to avoid peer pressure.

"My son, if sinful men entice you, does not give in to them. If they say, "Come along with us; let's lie in wait for innocent blood, let's ambush some harmless soul; let's swallow them alive, like the grave, and whole, like those who go down to the pit; we will get all sorts of valuable things and fill our houses with plunder; cast lots with us; we will all share the loot"— my son, do not go along with them, do not set foot on their paths" (Proverbs 1:10-15 NIV).

"Do not be misled: "Bad company corrupts good character" (1 Corinthians 15:33 NIV).

We must use wisdom and avoid those who want to lead us down the wrong path. We must avoid those who hold to bad morals and realize the power of influence. We must choose our friends wisely.

"Blessed is the one who does not walk in step with the wicked or stand in the way that sinners take or sit in the company of mockers, but whose delight is in the law of the LORD, and who meditates on his law day and night" (Psalms 1:1-2 NIV).

One thing I have always tried to do, I don't know if I have succeeded in this book or any of the others

I have written, and that is to tell us the "how". Many preachers, writers, teachers always want to tell us what is wrong, but they always seem to forget to tell us how to stay away from the wrong.

Dare

We need to dare to be different we need to dare to be right. We must have courage and conviction. It is easy to stand with the crowd and go along with them it is difficult and takes courage to stand alone. We have to make decisions ahead of time and know what our answer will be when the peer pressure is presented. When you face pressure and you take a stand alone, count it as an honor.

Desire

Make it your desire to keep your priorities in alignment with God. You have to ask yourself this question: "Do I want to be popular and accepted by men, or to be right with God?" We all need self-control, prayer, persistence and we must have a desire to surrender ourselves to God. We must develop the desire to gain approval from God and not from men.

STANDING IN AWE

The psalmist stated in verse 120, "My flesh trembles in fear of you; I stand in awe of your laws." Now when you or I read this we automatically think that we are supposed to be afraid of God and stand and tremble in His presence. I won't go into the phrase "fear of the Lord" because it was covered in my first book and you can read it there. The psalmist stated that he was in "awe" of God's Word. We have spent quite a few chapters on God's Word and now we are presented with another aspect of the way we look at God's Word.

There is a worship song that is very popular today and uses the words that I have used as the title of this chapter. The song is titled "Let My Words Be Few", and throughout the song we hear the phrase "oh I stand in awe of You, Jesus". When I hear this song, when I think of what the psalmist wrote, and when I see the lyrics of the above song a question enters into my mind asking "do I really stand in awe of God?"

Let's take a few minutes of my time and your time to investigate this subject. If you know the song above or even if you don't take the time to listen to it or sing it and then ask yourself, "do I really stand in awe of God?" "Do I live it, feel it, and actually do it?" "Is it possible in the world of today to know the awesomeness of God?" I think it is, but I have to write down on these pages, I really don't know the last time I have stood in awe of God.

Solomon who wrote the book of Proverbs and the book of Ecclesiastes made a lot of mistakes in his life, but he also knew what it was like to stand in awe of God. In the book of Ecclesiastes, he gives us some steps on how to stand in awe of God.

"Watch your step when you enter God's house. Enter to learn. That's far better than mindlessly offering a sacrifice, doing more harm than good.

Don't shoot off your mouth, or speak before you think. Don't be too quick to tell God what you think he wants to hear. God's in charge, not you—the less you speak, the better.

Overwork makes for restless sleep. Over talk shows you up as a fool.

When you tell God you'll do something, do it— now. God takes no pleasure in foolish gabble. Vow it, and then do it. Far better not to vow in the first place than to vow and not pay up.

Don't let your mouth make a total sinner of you. When called to account, you won't get by with 'Sorry, I didn't mean it.' Why risk provoking God to angry retaliation?

But against all illusion and fantasy and empty talk there's always this rock foundation: Fear God" (Ecclesiastes 5:1-7 MSG)!

Let's take a look at what Solomon is really saying to us. Sometimes I think we become too comfortable with God, we lose sight of how awesome God really is. Let's look at it this way. When you see a celebrity on TV or you recognize a famous author's name on a book, you feel a sort of awe. If you have the chance to get to know that celebrity or author and you find out who they really are you become more comfortable with them and you lose some of that awe because you see they are human. I will give you an example.

When my daughter was younger and I coached her soccer team we found out that a certain celebrity had a daughter who played on another team in the same town. This celebrity was Garth Brooks. That year when I coached we had a chance to meet him after a game and we literally stood in awe because after all he was Garth Brooks. When the next year rolled around his daughter and my daughter ended up on the same team, and quite a few years after they always were on the same team. He held practices out at his place, and at the end of each soccer season, he would put a party together for the girls and we all go out to his place. Through those years, I got to know him a little and he stood around with other parents and we all talked and became more comfortable with him. After some time, we still thought it was "awesome" to know Garth Brooks, but some of that "awe" had worn off. Why? Because we knew him on a more personal level, a more comfortable level than just seeing him on TV or listening to him on the radio.

God isn't human, He is divine, He is Almighty, yet I think at times we, including me, have become too comfortable with Him, and with His presence and we forget to stand in awe. So how do we overcome this struggle? Look at the verses above again and read them again and we will notice these steps.

First we have to GUARD our steps when we enter into God's house when we enter into the church. We also have to guard our steps before we get to God's house. Sometimes before you even get to church you fight over who is going to get into the shower first. You rush around looking for the right clothes to wear, you can't find the perfect socks, and the belt you wore last week has disappeared. You spill your coffee on the way out the door and it is cold outside, and now you have to spend time scraping the frost from the windows. Therefore, your mind and heart isn't ready for worship and you don't even have half a chance of standing in awe. Maybe those examples are not you. Maybe you have good intentions as the time of the service gets close, but then during the service, you can't seem to pay attention. Your thoughts drift away as the preacher reads the Word of God. During the sermon, you pass the time thinking about work, or you doodle on the bulletin, or you glance around the sanctuary, looking at others who might be taking a nap, or you are looking at the baby two rows up. If this is you, then the first thing is to be on guard.

Second we have to realize GOD is in charge. Not us. Sometimes we want to tell God what we think He wants to hear. We need to learn to think before we talk. Sometimes we need to LISTEN more than we need to talk. People who talk all the time become like a fool just as people who work too much become restless and lose sleep. Too many times, I think we get comfortable in life and we think we are in charge. When we pray we have a tendency to tell God what He must do.

Third we must FOLLOW through. Sometimes we talk and talk and talk, and we make promises to God and we don't follow through with those promises. We are told in the above verses that when we tell God we are going to do it then we must do it. If you make a promise, then keep it. We can't just say, "Sorry, I changed my mind, I didn't mean it." We make promises all the time to people and many times we break those promises because we are busy, or we forgot. In church sometimes we make promises to God in private by saying "God I will do this and that if you do so and so".

Fourth we must FEAR God. We have to be careful of empty talk, making promises we don't intend to keep. Solomon sums it all up at the end of Ecclesiastes when he tells us the duty of man is to "fear God and keep His commandments." The psalmist wanted to stand in awe of God and His Word; we should look at the Word of God with reverence and know that when God speaks with His Word we should obey.

SONG FROM THE HEART

We have just seen the song the psalmist was singing as he continued his traveling and the song is "to stand in awe of God" as noted in verse 120. The last time you read God's Word, the last time you entered the church, were you "AWE-STRUCK? When you, when I, read the Word we need to be struck with awe for God and His majesty, His power, and His might. When we find ourselves singing the song and the phrase, "Oh, I stand in AWE of You, Jesus", I pray that the phrase becomes a reality instead of a remark uttered out of habit.

"Once a spider built a beautiful web in an old house. He kept it clean and shiny so that flies would patronize it. The minute he got a "customer" he would clean up on him so the other flies would not get suspicious. Then one day this fairly intelligent fly came buzzing by the clean spider web. Old man spider called out, "Come in and sit." But the fairly intelligent fly said, "No, sir. I don't see other flies in your house, and I am not going in alone!"

But presently he saw on the floor below a large crowd of flies dancing around on a piece of brown paper. He was delighted! He was not afraid if lots of flies were doing it. So he came in for a landing. Just before he landed, a bee zoomed by, saying, "Don't land there, stupid! That's flypaper!" But the fairly intelligent fly shouted back, "Don't be silly. Those flies are dancing. There's a big crowd there. Everybody's doing it. That many flies can't be wrong!"

Well, you know what happened. He died on the spot. Some of us want to be with the crowd too badly that we end up in a mess. What does it profit a fly (or a person) if he escapes the web only to end up in the glue?" [52]

"Pictures of the Grand Canyon are amazing. When we lived in Phoenix, Arizona we went to see the Grand Canyon in person. When I stood at the edge of the canyon and looked out words cannot express the beauty, enormity, and creation of God's wonder. Pictures and words could never have conveyed what I saw and felt.

Many times we can read of God's splendor, grace, mercy, and power but very seldom do we "Stand In Awe Of God". If, just if, we could stand in awe of God we would not fear anything in our lives. We start to fear when we put God in the same intellectual capacity as us. How will God protect me when I am this far in the hole, or this sick or _____ " If we are not in Awe of God we will start to make God think like us instead of letting God be God." 53

OUR PRAYER

Heavenly Father, when I am tempted to compromise and fall to peer pressure, help me to stand firm on Your Word. Help me to constantly stand in awe of You and the Word of God. In Jesus name, Amen.

Song #16

"Enough is Enough"

"I've had all I can stand and I can't stands no more" 54
Popeye the Sailor Man

Psalms 119:121-128

¹²¹ *"I have done judgment and justice: leave me not to mine oppressors.*

¹²² *Be surety for thy servant for good: let not the proud oppress me.*

¹²³ *Mine eyes fail for thy salvation, and for the word of thy righteousness.*

¹²⁴ *Deal with thy servant according unto thy mercy, and teach me thy statutes.*

¹²⁵ *I am thy servant; give me understanding, that I may know thy testimonies.*

¹²⁶ *It is time for thee, LORD, to work: for they have made void thy law.*

¹²⁷ *Therefore I love thy commandments above gold; yea, above fine gold.*

¹²⁸ Therefore I esteem all thy precepts concerning all things to be right; and I hate every false way."

You might remember the Popeye cartoon or comic book. The character that "was strong to the finish because he ate his spinach". Popeye started out as a character in a comic strip. The character first made his theatrical appearance in 1933. The cartoon quickly became a fan favorite and pretty soon was passed into the hands of Paramount studios and they continued to produce the cartoon until 1957. The quote above was quoted in some of the cartoons when Popeye had enough of his foes.

The psalmist in chapter 119 has faced the same sentiments when he looks around and sees that he is still being oppressed by his oppressors and he speaks out to God and basically is saying "I've had all I can stand, and I can't stand it any longer". If we are honest, we all have been there. We all have said "enough is enough."

The 16th Hebrew letter is **AYIN**! This means eye in all regular senses, but also, can mean knowledge, and character. It also can mean spring or fountain. The eye produces water when grief or pain is processed. It deals with cleansing and purification.

Vs. 121-I have
    DONE what is right and just
    DO not leave me to my oppressors.

Vs. 122-Be on the
    SIDE of Your
    SERVANT, Lord
    GOD, do not let the arrogant and the
    GODLESS oppress me.

Vs. 123-My eyes are getting tired,
    LOOKING for Your salvation
    LOOKING for Your right promises.

Vs. 124-Let Your love
    DICTATE how you will
    DEAL with me
    TEACH me from Your
    TEXTBOOK.

Vs. 125-I am Your
    SERVANT
    GIVE me discernment
    GIVE me understanding of Your
    STATUTES.

Vs. 126-It's time for you to act
    LORD, Your
    LAW is
    BEING
    BROKEN.

Vs. 127-I love Your Word
    MORE than
    GOLD
    MORE than pure
    GOLD.

Vs. 128-Because I
    HONOR all of Your Word, I
    HATE every wrong path.

THE COMMON QUESTION

Why do the evil people prosper and the godly suffer? This has been the common, age-old question. Jeremiah had asked God this question, Solomon also spent times wondering the very same thing. Now, the psalmist is asking it as well. I have asked this question, you have asked this question. The psalmist had become frustrated in the very first verse of this section. We have all become frustrated and wonder how this happens and sometimes we say, "We have had enough, and we can't stand it any longer".

Remember as you are reading this book and reading the whole 119th chapter of Psalms, this is a continued prayer. Let's take a closer look at these verses and see what his prayer includes.

He prays for SECURITY! The psalmist in verse 121 says "Hey, I have done right, why are they still oppressing me?" We might be saying the same thing. I am living right, why am I having difficulties, and why are people mistreating me? We may never really understand why, our minds may never comprehend the reasons why, but we should always remember God has never left us alone. We have God's grace, and we will find that God's grace is "sufficient" and God's strength is made perfect in our weakness. In all of our difficulties, persecutions, and trials we need to keep our hearts open to God's Word and God's way.

Next, he prays for SURETY. In verse 122, he wants God to be on his side, to "ensure" his well- being. The psalmist knows that he had done what is right, so he wants a guarantee that the arrogant and evil ones do not continue to oppress him. The word "surety" means to have security against loss or damage it also means to have a guarantee. He doesn't tell God how to take care of the oppressors; he leaves that part up to God.

He also prays for SALVATION. In verse 123 he states that his eyes are getting tired waiting, so he prays for salvation from the Lord. This salvation is rescue. When we look around at our difficult circumstances, sometimes we get tired, our eyes get tired of looking at all the problems, and yet we do not pray for salvation, we simply keep our eyes focused on the problems instead of keeping our eyes focused on God.

IT'S TIME FOR ACTION

The psalmist continues his prayer in verses 124 and 125 asking God to teach him the Word. If we take a few moments to remember back to the last 3 chapters of this book we talked a lot about the Word of God and how we should treat it. Here we get the idea that if we are reading God's Word and studying it, then we should ask God to teach us things from it. The psalmist actually uses these phrases, "teach me", "give me discernment" and "help me understand" the Word. Then he gives a bold proclamation to God, he says, "It is time for You to act, God!" Then he gives the reason why he is asking this of God and that reason is because the law of God is being broken, in another version, he says, "Your revelation is in shambles." These people that have continued to oppress and cause trouble have pushed God's Word to the side, they have pushed God out of their realm of living, and they have broken God's laws.

Does this sound like what is going on today in our society? People around us, the world around us have continued to push God's Word to the back burner some have even pushed it completely off the stove. It is time for God to act! It is time for the Christians to pray and ask God to act. There are three possible actions that might take place when we call on God to act, and they are Revival,

Ruin or the Rapture. God might bring revival and a spiritual awakening in this time of wickedness and apathy. He might bring a devastating ruin either socially or economically. He might rapture out the church from this evil world.

I read these two statements the other day and I liked them so much I want to share them with you. "The more the world sets aside the Word of God the more believers should cherish and hold dear to it." "The more the world ignores it, the more we should submit to it." 55

PURE GOLD

The psalmist finishes up this section by telling us he loves God's Word more than gold, but not just gold, pure gold. We notice once again, the psalmist is in love with God's Word. He puts a monetary value on the Word of God. He loves and desires God's Word more than the world and its wealth.

Three things that the Word of God can do for us that wealth cannot do for us.

Wealth cannot give us perseverance in our trials or courage at the time of death, but the Word of

God enables our souls to find strength in troubles and we can welcome death with the highest degree of courage. The Word of God is a greater and higher investment.

Wealth cannot give us the enjoyment of having a loving spirit or a clear conscience, but the Word of God can teach us how to love and how to keep a clear conscience and to have a friendship with God. The Word of God gives us a higher joy.

Wealth cannot give us or form a connection to heaven it cannot buy us a ticket for admission into heaven. Wealth cannot give us peace and cannot abide inside of us. The Word of God abides in us, it is our light, and it is our place of solace. The Word of God teaches us the only way to heaven is through God the Father. The Word of God gives us a higher hope.

In verse 128, the psalmist puts a moral value on the Word of God. He tells us that God's Word is always right, whether we understand it or believe it. God's Word is absolute truth. Since it is the truth, we need to believe it, but as Christians, we should not worry so much if we believe it but rather worry about if we obey it. God's Word is worth investing our lives in. God's work is worth our investment as well.

SONG FROM THE HEART

The psalmist writes in verse 126 "It is time for You to act Lord because they are breaking Your laws." We have mentioned at the beginning of this chapter and we have all probably thought what the psalmist has said, and we have been frustrated. We must take into account what the Apostle Paul has said when he tells the people of Galatia *"Do not be deceived: God is not mocked, for whatever one sows, that will he also reap."*

Many times we get frustrated and we think that God is not doing anything. We should pray for those who seem to prosper, and pray that they come to repentance instead of being frustrated by what we see in their lives. In this life, their prosperity will be just temporary, but we can look at our life and know that we will have eternal riches with God.

"Notwithstanding many "wets" declare that Prohibition does not prohibit, hundreds of prisons throughout the United States contain evidence to the contrary. "Whatsoever a man soweth, that shall he also reap."

273

In a certain State in the Union, a millionaire was engaged in the bootlegging business, thinking it an easy way to increase his wealth. He now undoubtedly believes the verse quoted above, for he is at the present time serving a long term in prison. A friend who called on him within the prison walls found him working, sitting cross-legged, with a big needle and a ball of twine. Sewing burlap bags. The friend, not knowing what else to say, remarked, "Sewing, eh?" Looking up with an ill-natured smile, the man replied, "No; I'm reaping." 56

"The Bible is a book beyond all books as a river is above and beyond a rivulet. The Bible is a book beyond all books as the sun is above and beyond a candle in brightness. The Bible is a book beyond all books as the wings of an eagle is above and beyond the wings of a sparrow. It is supernatural in origin, eternal in duration, inexpressible in value, immeasurable in influence, infinite in scope, divine in authorship, human in penmanship, regenerative in power, infallible in authority, universal in interest, personal in application, and inspired in totality. This is the Book that has walked more paths, traveled more highways, knocked at more doors and spoken to more people in their mother tongue than in other books this world has ever known or will know." 57

OUR PRAYER

Heavenly Father please forgive us of our sins, and help those who do not know You to repent of their sin. We know that You withhold judgment so that others will repent. We thank you for your great mercy. Help us to see God's Word is better than pure gold. In Jesus Name, Amen.

Song #17

"The River of Tears"

"Tears shed for self are tears of weakness,
but tears shed for others are a sign of strength."[58]
Billy Graham

Psalms 119:129-136

[129] *"Thy testimonies are wonderful: therefore doth my soul keep them.*

[130] *The entrance of thy words giveth light; it giveth understanding unto the simple.*

[131] *I opened my mouth, and panted: for I longed for thy commandments.*

[132] *Look thou upon me, and be merciful unto me, as thou usest to do unto those that love thy name.*

[133] *Order my steps in thy word: and let not any iniquity have dominion over me.*

[134] *Deliver me from the oppression of man: so will I keep thy precepts.*

[135] *Make thy face to shine upon thy servant; and teach me thy statutes.*

136 Rivers of waters run down mine eyes, because they keep not thy law."

The psalmist has traveled many miles by this point in the chapter, and he has seen a lot of different things, he's dealt with oppressors from all sides, he's dealt with his own troubles, he's been on an emotional roller coaster, but he has seen many who do not follow the Word of God and he stops and cries for those who are not following. As I was reading these eight verses, verse 136 stuck out to me. I was thinking about the world in which we live and how we are taught many times to become calloused and we are taught that it is weak to cry. But when we are crying from the heart, I believe that is commendable. I am not talking about the fake tears we might see from Hollywood or the selfish tears we see from someone wallowing around in self-pity. I am talking about tears from the heart towards God when we hear the song "Amazing grace how sweet the sound, that saved a wretch like me; I once was lost, but now I'm found, was blind but now I see." I am talking about tears from the heart towards God when we hear someone speak against God and mock His Holy name. When is the last time you cried a river of tears for someone you know who does not have a relationship with Jesus Christ?

The next letter in the Hebrew alphabet is **PE**! The word *peh* means mouth, but it is associated with speech. Some say the shape of the letter looks like a face with a mouth.

Vs. 129- Your
      WORD is
      WONDERFUL, how cannot I not obey?

Vs. 130-Opening Your Word
      GIVES light, opening Your Word
      GIVES understanding to the naïve.

Vs. 131-I open my
      MOUTH and pant, I want Your Word
      MORE than anything.

Vs. 132-Have mercy on me and
      LOOK kindly on me, for those who
      LOVE Your Name, You always do

Vs. 133-STEADY my
      STEPS according to your Word, let no
      SIN rule over me.

Vs. 134-Rescue me from human
OPPRESSION, so I will
OBEY Your Word.

Vs. 135-SHINE down on me,
SMILE down on Your
SERVANT. Teach me Your Word.

Vs. 136-Rivers of tears I cry
BECAUSE nobody is living
BY Your
BOOK!

WHAT IS YOUR OPINION?

If there is anything that you have noticed about this book, and about Psalms 119, I and the psalmist keep stressing how important the Word of God is. I don't know what your opinion is on the Word of God, but here we read the opinion of the psalmist in verse 129. He says, "The Word is Wonderful." He believes that it is so wonderful that he can't help but do what the Word says to do, he must obey it.

There are some who will probably disagree but if you consider the Bible to be a great book, then your consideration would be correct. The Bible has been translated into numerous languages and is still one of the best-selling books of all time. If you consider the Bible to be a treasure, then your consideration would be correct. It is an ancient book, written by many authors over a period of centuries. It has been copied and preserved and passed down from generation to generation. There have been many people who have literally given their lives so that we can have a Bible or a copy to read in our own language. But, if we become like the psalmist and say the Bible is a "wonderful book, therefore I will obey it", then we have made a greater statement. If we read the Bible and do not obey it, then we have read a great book, we have read a great treasure from the past. But if we read the Word of God and obey the words written therein, then we are transformed, we are changed, and we honor and glorify God.

There is a website called Debate.org and the question has been posed "Is the Bible really the Word of God?" There are many different responses and I will share two of them here. The poll at the top of the website page shows 44% say "yes" it is, and 56% say "no" it isn't.

"The Bible posits that the Abrahamic God has specific attributes, among them being: Omniscience (all-knowing) and omnipotence (all-powerful).

If one believes the Bible is the word of god, it must follow that...

...This all-knowing and all-powerful deity decides to write a book, to communicate His existence and His glory to the world, and let His people know what they have to do to avoid what he will do to them if they don't do what he puts in his book. So he sits down and writes--- oh, wait. He leans down and speaks the words of the Biblical texts into the waiting and diligent ears of mostly illiterate bronze-age tribesmen, who either write it down immediately, or pass it on by word of mouth for several hundred years. Then, this all-knowing and all-powerful deity simply stands by while his clumsy humans lose all the original documents and several generations to follow, and muddle up which books were "really" God-inspired and which were forgeries. All-knowing and all-powerful god *does nothing to clarify anything. Instead, he chooses right about the time the printing press was developed to slow down the "miracle" business, stopping entirely after the invention of the video camera.*

The facts are this: We don't have the original Biblical texts. The texts we do have don't agree with each other. The Biblical version of history doesn't line up with actual history, to say nothing of its idea of the natural sciences and mathematics. There is no reason to believe that the Bible is authored by a deity who is described in said book as all-knowing and all-powerful." 59

"The fact that God gave us the Bible is an evidence and illustration of His love for us. The term "revelation" simply means that God communicated to mankind what He is like and how we can have a right relationship with Him. These are things that we could not have known had God not divinely revealed them to us in the Bible. Although God's revelation of Himself in the Bible was given progressively over approximately 1500 years, it has always contained everything man needs to know about God in order to have a

right relationship with Him. If the Bible is truly the Word of God, then it is the final authority for all matters of faith, religious practice, and morals.

The question we must ask ourselves is how can we know that the Bible is the Word of God and not just a good book? What is unique about the Bible that sets it apart from all other religious books ever written? Is there any evidence that the Bible is truly God's Word? These types of questions must be seriously examined if we are to determine the validity of the Bible's claim to be the very Word of God, divinely inspired, and totally sufficient for all matters of faith and practice. There can be no doubt that the Bible does claim to be the very Word of God. This is clearly seen in Paul's commendation to Timothy: "... from infancy you have known the holy Scriptures, which are able to make you wise for salvation through faith in Christ Jesus. All Scripture is God-breathed and is useful for teaching, rebuking, correcting and training in righteousness, so that the man of God may be thoroughly equipped for every good work" (2 Timothy 3:15-17).

There are both internal and external evidences that the Bible is truly God's Word. The internal evidences are those things within the Bible that testify of its divine origin. One of the first internal evidences that the Bible is truly God's Word is seen in its unity. Even though it is really sixty-six individual books, written on three continents, in three different languages, over a period of approximately 1500 years, by more than 40 authors who came from many walks of life, the Bible remains one unified book from beginning to end without contradiction. This unity is unique from all other books and is evidence of the divine origin of the words which God moved men to record." [60]

God's Word is wonderful, and we should strive to live by the words written therein, and we should strive to share those words with people in whom we come in contact.

Taking a look at the wonderful Word of God, let's take some time and look at how the psalmist noticed and how we should take notice of how wonderful the Word of God really is.

First, it is WONDERFUL IN ITS SUFFICIENCY. The Word of God is the instruction manual for life. You have always heard "When all else fails, read the instructions." God's wisdom is revealed to us through each chapter and verse. We don't need to add to it or try to remove anything from the pages of the Bible. The Bible is everything we need. Throughout the pages we have God's promises; we have instructions and commands on how we should live.

"His divine power has given us everything we need for a godly life through our knowledge of him who called us by his own glory and goodness. Through these he has given us his very great and precious promises, so that through them you may participate in the divine nature, having escaped the corruption in the world caused by evil desires" (2 Peter 1:3-4 NIV).

Secondly, it is WONDERFUL IN ITS SIMPLICITY. God's Word is not hard to understand, even though there are many that believe it is. We have to study and read, and the more we do this, the easier it is to understand. Now I could go into the different translations here and I won't take the time to do that, but if you will notice throughout my book I use scripture from the King James Version, New International Version, and the Message Bible. I believe you should find a version that you understand and enjoy reading. There are always controversies on which is the right version, but if you take the Word of God in whatever version, it is still God's Word and God can use any version to reach the minds and hearts of people. The Word of God is so simple that even children can understand the words. The basics of the Word are this: God tells us what we need to do; He then tells us what will happen if we fail to do it and if we follow it. He tells us how to deal with failure, and He tells us how to avoid making the same mistakes again and again.

"All Scripture is God-breathed and is useful for teaching, rebuking, correcting and training in righteousness, so that the servant of God may be thoroughly equipped for every good work" (2 Timothy 3:16-17 NIV).

Third, it is WONDERFUL IN ITS SUPPLY. God supplies our needs, but here the psalmist reminds us that God's Word brings with it certain benefits, and they are light and understanding. Both of these things have been supplied for our benefit.

We can choose to live in the light of His Word, or we can continue to walk in darkness. The psalmist tells us that the Bible can illuminate our lives. It can show us where we are spiritually and it can point us in the direction we need to go. It also is telling us on how to live. The word "simple" implies that at times we are all naïve. There are some who believe they are too intelligent to be taught by the Bible. But, in the end, we will find that the simplest person who puts their trust in God and in His Word will be more highly exalted than those with the greatest minds but have not trusted God.

STEADY STEPS

In verse 133, the psalmist prays that his steps are steady and directed by God and that sin doesn't rule over his life. This should be a prayer for all of us, for our families, friends, co-workers, and acquaintances.

As I continue to write this book, at the present moment I am actually one week from entering into the New Year of 2016. Every year when we enter into the New Year resolutions are made ranging from attitudes to actions. Some resolutions last while some do not make it very far into the year.

As we pray and as we walk into the New Year, we must realize that our steps need to be steady and directed. When we started out in life, whether that has been years ago, or just a few years ago, we all had to learn to walk, and throughout the journey of learning how to walk many times we fell down. To be able to walk requires an action of having the ability to move from one point to another. As we learned to walk we also learned to coordinate our movements and learned to move at various speeds including walking, jogging, running, skipping and sometimes limping. Whichever speed you have chosen to use they all required one basic element and that is to move one step at a time. Whether you are running a marathon, a 5k, a relay, a short jog around the block or a walk across your living room, each one requires the ability to take one step at a time. The reality of this principle was spoken by Neil Armstrong when he spoke the words "one small step for man, one giant leap for mankind."

Walking is a cherished movement that many of us possess, but there are others that do not have that ability. There is another type of walk that we all need and that is the ability to walk in the Word of God. The psalmist was traveling and walking and asked God to direct his steps or to steady his feet on the road in which he was traveling. There are other examples in the Word of God of men who had walked with God. Enoch walked with God, Peter had walked on the water towards Christ. Both men had taken one step at a time and their steps were directed by God. Each person in the Word of God who walked towards God allowed God to direct his steps. This is the prayer of the psalmist, that as he traveled and walked along his journey that all his steps would be directed by God and that sin would not rule over him.

If you have ever seen the movie "Chariots of Fire", you know that it was based on a true story of two athletes who were runners in the 1924 Olympics. The story follows two men, Eric Liddell, and Harold Abrahams. Eric Liddell who was a devout Scottish Christian ran for the glory of God. Harold Abrahams who was an English Jew ran to overcome prejudice. In the movie, Eric Liddell misses a church service because he was out running and he was accused by his sister of no longer caring about God. Eric feels inspired when he runs and told his sister, "I believe that God made me for a purpose. But He also made me fast, and when I run, I feel His pleasure."

He believed his steps were directed by God and he found pleasure in running for God. If we are followers of Christ we need to take the same attitude as Erick Liddell and take pleasure in walking or running after God and God's Word. Why? So that sin would no longer have dominion and rule over us.

The psalmist prayer was to always walk in the way of God, to make sure his steps were one at a time and that his steps were steady. He chose to live his life according to God's Word so that sin would not rule his life. Sin has a tendency to eat away at our life and our character and eventually can destroy us and we will crumble.

In a small town in Kansas many years ago, the residents had gathered in the high school gym for a basketball game. The game was going really well and the home team was supported by the stomping, clapping and cheering of the spectators. Something at halftime changed the town forever. As the fans were waiting for halftime to be over the gym was suddenly rocked by a powerful explosion. Everyone ran outside to see what had happened. The town's massive grain elevator had collapsed and had fallen on top of a small nursery school. Five little children died that day. What would have caused such a disaster? When the inspectors came and inspected the grain elevator's foundation, they discovered that termites had eaten the middle of the beams and rafters, leaving only a deceptive, empty shell. The damage had been done by the termites and it was hard to detect because they were working on the inside of the wood.

Termites (sin) work on the soul as well. Things can look good on the outside, but on the inside sin is slowly but surely destroying the person from the inside. You usually don't see termites out in the open they work in the dark, and carry small bits of wood away at a time. Sin works the same way, inside of a person we don't always see the sin, and it is eroding the soul bit by bit, a little at a time until they are totally destroyed. Termites are deceptive constantly destroying while no one is watching. Sin is deceptive as well destroying someone and no one sees what is going on. Termite damage doesn't happen overnight, they work steadily, but slowly. Sin doesn't always happen overnight, but it works steady and slowly taking it's time to destroy.

We can get rid of the termites of sin if we continue to stay in God's Word because it is powerful and we can get rid of the termites of sin is we pray as the psalmist did and allow the Lord to direct our steps and to not let sin rule over us.

RIVER OF TEARS

In verse 136 the psalmist says he "cries a river of tears because people are not following the Word." We see people living against the Word of God every day and we see people who have a complete disregard for the Word of God. There is a video on YouTube where the comedian George Carlin is talking about religion. He obviously is an atheist and his complete disregard for God is appalling. In the video, he tells how God is an incompetent God because of the things that have happened in the world in which we live. Another person who has some videos out about religion and the Bible is Ricky Gervaise, and he also spends time mocking God when he reads from the Bible. Most Christians get really upset at this mockery, and the things that these men have said, and many times we just get mad and leave it at that, believing we can't do anything about it. We have a friend who is a good friend to our daughter, but he also comes over to the house and spends time with us. This young man claims to be an atheist and we have talked back and forth and we completely disagree with each other when it comes to Christianity, and there have been times in the middle of a discussion where I become angry and mad at his thoughts and his words.

One thing I noticed when I was reading this psalm is the psalmist wept over those who had a complete disregard for God's laws. I believe Christians spend more time trying to pick battles with people who do not believe and we constantly try to prove that we are right, when in reality we should be going to prayer for these people and weeping over their souls.

I believe God wants us to get into the habit of crying over lost souls and maintaining a tender heart of compassion and love towards others. The question for me and the question for you is "Why don't we cry for the lost?"

I think we don't cry for the lost because we are not BURDENED for their souls. I believe that apathy and indifference have become one of the greatest hindrances to having a burden for people. Our hearts are cold and calloused about the eternal destiny of others. We are so involved in this busy world that we neglect prayer and neglect telling others about Christ. We just don't feel a burden for the lost any longer. How should we be burdened for these lost? First, I think we need a burden to PRAY CONTINUALLY. Most of the time when we pray for someone to be saved, we pray for a couple of weeks or maybe a couple of months, and we give up if they don't get saved.

There was a football coach who showed his players several films of football games to get his players inspired. In one of the films, there was this big guy who hit another player and slammed him to the ground. The player who got hit just lay there and finally got up and limped off the field. In another film, there was that same big guy who hit another player and slammed him to the ground. But the player that got hit, jumped up. The very next play the big guy slammed him to the ground again, the player jumped up. This went on play after play. Finally, the coach said to his players, "Now which player do we want on our team?" The enthusiastic players responded in unison, "The guy who keeps jumping up!" The coach replied, "NO! We want that big guy doing all that slamming down!"

We can't be like the big guy when it comes to prayer, but we can be persistent.

Second, we need to have a burden to PRAY CHRIST-LIKE. Jesus instructs us about our attitude of prayer; we should seek to forgive others as we ourselves seek forgiveness. There are some Christians who won't pray for some to be saved simply because they do not like them. Richard Weaver, a Christian, earned his living in the mines. He had the higher priority; however, he was always trying to bring his work associates to the Savior and to God's Word. While most of the men were indifferent, one became offended by his witness, and finally said, "I'm sick of your constant preaching. I've a good mind to punch you in the face!" "Go ahead if it will make you feel better," answered Weaver. The man immediately struck him with a stinging blow. Weaver did not retaliate but turned the other cheek. Again the man struck him in the face and walked away cursing under his breath. Weaver shouted, "I forgive you, and I still pray to the Lord that He will save you!" The next morning the assailant was waiting for him when he came to work "Oh, Dick," he said, his voice filled with emotion, "do you really forgive me for what I did yesterday?" "Certainly", said Weaver extending his hand. As he told him again the message of salvation, God opened the man's heart, and he received Christ.

We should also have a burden to PRAY CORRECTLY. When we are praying we should pray for the souls of others, they must be our priority in prayer. When we are burdened for them, we should always pray for them by name.

Next, I don't think we pray for lost souls because we are not BROKEN. I think there are a lot of times we are not broken over the lost souls of people because we let irritation with how they believe come to the forefront of our minds. First I believe we need to be BROKEN OVER OURSELVES. In Isaiah 6 we notice where Isaiah becomes broken over himself. He said, "Woe is me, for I am undone; I am a man of unclean lips, and I dwell in the midst of a people unclean lips." Isaiah recognized his own sin, and he trembled and knelt in repentance and humility. If we are to tell others about Jesus Christ, we must have a clean soul.

Second, we need to be BROKEN OVER SOULS. After Isaiah got himself right with God, then he became concerned about others. He heard the Lord speak, "Whom shall I send, and who will go for us? Isaiah answered and said, "Here am I; send me."

There was a slogan many years ago concerning letting people drive drunk and the slogan was, "Friends Don't Let Friends Drive Drunk." It became a very popular slogan and I have seen it quite a bit as a commercial on TV. If you think of that slogan, we can move it over to the spiritual world and say, "Friends Don't Let Friends Die

Lost". Can we say that? Would we use that as a slogan to spur us to witness? If you had a friend or neighbor and their house caught on fire, would you grab a hose, or run to the house and make sure they were out while waiting on the fire truck? If you had a cure for a terrible disease would you keep it to yourself, or would you share it with those who needed it? Yet, we have people dying around us and they have a terrible disease of sin, and we have the cure, yet we don't share it.

I pray as I am writing this that I will be broken over the atheist who refuses to see God. I pray as I am writing this that I will be broken over the friend at work who doesn't know Jesus. I pray for the family member who has refused the Word of God many times. I pray that I will become like the psalmist and weep over those who do not know Jesus.

SONG FROM THE HEART

The Word of God is powerful and yet there are many who continue to break the law of God. We should not become angry with those people, but we should pray for them and pray for ourselves to cry rivers of tears over their lost soul. The psalmist song was found in verse 136 when he says "I cry rivers of tears because nobody is living by Your book."

We never know when we are going to step out of this world into eternity, and we don't know when people around us are going to leave this world. We must shed tears for the lost, but we also must point them to the cross with our words and our actions. Theodore Roosevelt said, **"People don't care how much you know until they know how much you care"!** 61

Billy Moore grew up in a rough city in Ohio to an impoverished family. He got involved with crime when he was young. He took drug and would get drunk and break into taverns and steal cash from the registers – and committed all kinds of petty theft. Then he joined the army, got married. His wife left him took their kid with her. He was broke, and he was desperate.

One night he and a friend were drinking, and doing drugs, and talking about how broke they were. His friend said, "I know about a guy who lives not too far from here, and the word is, he doesn't trust banks. He keeps all his money in his bedroom." Billy said, "Is he some big, tough guy?" And the friend said, "No, he's an old guy. Wouldn't hurt a flea."

So the plot hatched in Billy's mind. He went back to

the barracks, got his gun, and loaded it. He drove to that man's house, broke in, and started ransacking the house.

The 77 years old man hears the noise and gets his shotgun he used for hunting. As Billy Moore breaks through the door of the bedroom and comes through the door with a gun in his hand, this elderly gentleman pointed his shotgun, pulled the trigger, and a blast went off. The buckshot went over Billy's head, missed him completely. Billy took his gun, pointed it at the old man, and he pulled the trigger twice. The elderly gentleman fell dead. Billy rifled through the man's clothes and bedroom and walked away with $5,600 in cash. He fled to his trailer in rural Georgia. It didn't take long for the police to track him down. They arrested him and took him to jail. You can imagine his first night in jail. He realizes his life is over. He's charged with capital murder. There's an electric chair waiting for him.

Billy Moore's mom was a Christian, and she knew a Christian couple who lived not far from the jail in Georgia. She called and said, "I got a son, and he's on death row. Would you please go visit him?" They went to visit Billy Moore, and they said to Billy, "Jesus is willing to give you a fresh start and a new chance at life." Billy looked back at them dumbfounded and said, "You got to be kidding me. Don't you realize my situation here? I murdered an old grandfather. I am charged with a death penalty case. My life is over.

There are no new beginnings for me." But that Christian man looked back at Billy Moore and said, "No, you don't understand. Jesus Christ loves you so much he wants to find a way to make your life count." Billy not only heard these words from this man and woman, but he saw Jesus in them. He said later, "Nobody ever told me Jesus had died for me. It was a love I could feel. It was a love I wanted. It was a love I needed."

Billy Moore, being hopeless and broken got on his knees in his jail cell and prayed: "God, I'm sorry for all I've done, and I want to live for you. If you would adopt me and take me to heaven, that would be the best. I don't have much time left, but if you could do something to make my life count, it would be like icing on the cake."

Jesus heard that prayer. There was a bathtub there on death row. They got permission from the guards to fill it up with water. Billy Moore knelt in the bathtub, and they dipped him backward into the water to baptize him.

God began to change Billy from the inside out. Billy went to court and pleaded guilty. He said, "How can I tell you I didn't do it when I did?" They found him guilty and sentenced him to death. But the criminal justice system is slow. It took 16 years of living in a cage waiting to die, but during those 16 years, Billy opened his life up to God.

Billy Moore became a model prisoner, so much so that the guards had a nickname for him. They called him "the peacemaker." Death row was an ugly, violent, hateful place until Billy got there. Bill had Bible studies with the other inmates, and one by one they found redemption and new life in Jesus Christ. The place that had been awful and violent became a place of hope where people cared for each other.

In 1990, the court system finally caught up with Billy Moore. The hours were ticking down to August 22 when they would put him to death. The lawyers were asked what it was like to talk to a man days before his death. The lawyers said that talking to Billy Moore was the strangest experience they ever had. "We would call to console him, but he ended up consoling us. Bill would say things like, 'Are you guys okay? I know this is difficult for you. Can I pray for you? We were trying to reach out to him, and he was reaching out to us. Why?" Because Billy Moore was no afraid to meet Jesus Christ face to face. He wasn't afraid because he knew Jesus as His Lord and Savior.

On August 21st, 1990, seven and a half hours before Billy Moore was to be electrocuted, something amazing happened. In fact, it's unprecedented in American history. The Georgia Pardon and Parole Board held an emergency hearing about a model prisoner they'd heard about. The five members of the Pardon and Parole Board looked at lifestyle and testimony of Billy Moore and did something so amazing it made the front page of the New York Times. They looked at Billy Moore and said, "We are going to show you mercy." They threw out the death penalty against Billy Moore and did something that had never been done in American history: they set the gears in motion to release him from prison. After he was released from prison, Billy Moore went on to be a minister. 62

OUR PRAYER

Heavenly Father, we pray today that we would have steady steps directed by You. We pray and ask that You help us as we walk for You and that sin would not have any rule over us. Help us to realize how wonderful the Word of God is, and help us to share it with our friends and neighbors and to weep for those who need You. In Jesus Name, Amen.

Song #18

"Consumed by Passion"

"Without passion man is a mere latent force and possibility, like the flint which awaits the shock of the iron before it can give forth its spark." [63]
Henri Frederic Amiel

Psalms 119:137-144

[137] *"Righteous art thou, O LORD, and upright are thy judgments.*

[138] *Thy testimonies that thou hast commanded are righteous and very faithful.*

[139] *My zeal hath consumed me, because mine enemies have forgotten thy words.*

[140] *Thy word is very pure: therefore thy servant loveth it.*

[141] *I am small and despised: yet do not I forget thy precepts.*

[142] *Thy righteousness is an everlasting righteousness, and thy law is the truth.*

[143] *Trouble and anguish have taken hold on me: yet thy commandments are my delights.*

[144] *The righteousness of thy testimonies is everlasting: give me understanding, and I shall live."*

In a previous chapter, we looked at what our opinion is concerning the Word of God and our opinion on whether we believe the Bible is the true Word of God. Here we see it again, as the psalmist uses the words "give me understanding that I may live." If the Bible is the authentic Word of God and if the Bible is the truth, then it contains the truth about the way we should live our lives. If we believe the Bible is the Word of God then we should live our lives by its teachings, and we need to take immediate action. We must study it and know what it says, we have to apply it to our everyday lives and relate it to our lives so we can handle any circumstance that comes our way in this life. The psalmist also notices again like in the last chapter that his enemies had a complete disregard for the Word of God and so he becomes consumed with zeal or passion for the Word of God. In this chapter, we will look at passion and the Word of God and see if we are consumed by a passion for God.

The Hebrew letter in this section is **TSADHE** and it is the 18th letter of the Hebrew alphabet. Some believe that the verb *sud* means to hunt, and says that it means "fish hook." Another name for this letter is *saddiq*, meaning just, or righteous.

Vs. 137-You are
RIGHTEOUS Lord and Your Word is
RIGHT.

Vs. 138-Your Word has been
APPOINTED as righteous and in
ALL faithfulness.

Vs. 139-Consumed by passion because my
FOES
FORGET Your Word.

Vs. 140-Your Word has been
THOROUGHLY
TESTED, and
YOUR servant loves
YOUR Word.

Vs. 141-Though I am small and
DESPISED, I
DO not forget Your Word.

Vs. 142-YOUR righteousness is everlasting
    YOUR Word is truth.

Vs. 143-Trouble and anguish have
    COME upon me but Your
    COMMANDMENTS are my delight.

Vs. 144-Your
    WORD is always right, Your
    WORD
    I need understanding so
    I may live.

PASSION

Many of us and many Christians have a passion for different things. Maybe we have a passion for football, baseball or some other sports team. Maybe we have a passion for guns, for cars, or movies. We are passionate about certain things but we need to have a passion for God's Word. The writer's passion grew more for God's Word because his enemies despised God's Word.

Why don't we have a passion for God's Word?

Excuse #1-STUFF OUR SOULS WITH SMALL THINGS.

One thing I am guilty of and many of us are guilty of we have a passion about things when compared to eternity doesn't make any difference in our lives. As we have embarked upon the New Year we will probably make some kind of resolve to do something better or do something more. Another thing we are guilty of including me is spending time on these "so-called" passions we have, but we find it hard to spend any time in God's Word. Think about it with me for just a moment. We will watch a football game for 3 to 4 hours and get real passionate over our team. We will go to the movies and sit and watch the movie for 2 hours or more. We will get deeply involved into a book that we find interesting and read it for days without putting it down. We will spend hours on Facebook or Twitter, chatting with people or posting our favorite meal or complaining about our jobs and read other posts for hours or play games on the computer for a few hours. Yet we have a hard time sitting down for 15 minutes and reading the Word of God. We need to have a hunger for God's Word we need to find some degree of hunger and passion. We will stuff our souls with small things.

Many guys can know all the NBA stats, the NFL stats on certain players, we spend hours looking at our fantasy football, but we know nothing about the Word of God. Many women can know the best purse to buy, where to get the best shoes, and know what stores offer 50% off, but yet have no idea what the Word of God says.

On average, a Bible will have approximately 1100 pages or more. Depending on what version, what typesetting the Bible is printed in will determine how many pages there are. If you were to take a Bible with 1500-1800 pages and you read 5 pages a day, you could read the Bible in one year. Most people shy away from the Old Testament because they find it difficult to read. The Old Testament to some people is like having that weird uncle or weird relative that we don't want to spend time with.

Excuse #2-WE ARE NOT A BIG READER

Maybe your excuse for not reading the Word of God is because you are not a big reader. You have never been a big reader, maybe the last time you read a book was because you had to read one for school. I am an avid reader, matter of fact, my daughter, and son-in-law just bought a book for me for Christmas and it is about finding Jesus in the Old Testament. Some people growing up and going through school pride themselves on not being a big reader. Understand this about the Bible, it is not a bunch of rules or an archaic book that traces the history of a bunch of people, it is not an almanac you consult when checking on a certain condition. The Bible is a bunch of love letters written from God. Some of you might remember getting love letters from a girlfriend or boyfriend. I don't think that happens as much today because of all the phones and computers where we can send text and messages quicker than writing a letter out by hand and waiting for the mailman to bring it. But if you have ever received a love letter from someone you loved or they loved you, then you probably read that letter and re-read that letter, and then read it again, and again until you almost had it memorized. Yet we can't stand to open up the Word of God and read the love letter He has given to us.

If you and your family go out to a restaurant in the next few days or weeks, and when you are seated you are handed a menu. You pick the menu up and by reading it you know what is cooking in the kitchen. When you pick up the menu, though, you don't just look over it and scan it and then put it back down and leave the restaurant. Why? Because you are not satisfied just by looking at the menu, you want to order food from it and you want to taste the food, then you are satisfied, well, we hope you are. Yet, we have the Bible and most of us treat it like the menu, we look at it, then put it down and walk away but yet we are not satisfied. The Bible tells us what is cooking in the kitchen, we need to read it, taste it, and be satisfied.

Excuse #3-IT IS HARD TO UNDERSTAND

You believe the Bible is hard to understand it's too much to take in. I think it is the way we approach the reading of it. Sometimes it is hard for us to be reading it alone. We need to read it with others in a Bible Study, a Sunday school, or with our spouse or children. Reading the Bible in a community setting is better than reading it all by ourselves. When we read it together with others we can learn together, have dialogue and discuss what we have read and it will help guard against goofy interpretations.

So how do we get re-ignited with a passion for reading God's Word? How do we move from reading because we feel obligated rather than reading for delight?

First, GROW DEEPER IN LOVE WITH THE AUTHOR. I have already mentioned this above but if a young woman received a love letter from her fiancée, she would eagerly read it because she is in love with the author of the letter. She would read it over and over, so she could discover the full meaning of her lover's message. Similarly, if we love God, we will want to read and re-read God's love letter to us and discover the full meaning of the letter. We would find delight in the inspired words of God.

"I seek you with all my heart;
 do not let me stray from your commands.
I have hidden your word in my heart
 that I might not sin against you" (Psalms 119:10-11 NIV).

Second, GET CLOSER TO GOD BY HAVING A PERSONAL RELATIONSHIP WITH THE AUTHOR. Since, God is the author of the Bible, the reader (us) should strive to truly know God through Jesus Christ. We need to develop and fortify our personal relationship with God. The relationship with God should be a deep and intimate relationship. If you and I truly know God and desire to have a close relationship with God, we will be more prepared to be joyful when we read and study God's Word.

"And this is eternal life, that they know you the only true God, and Jesus Christ whom you have sent" (John 17:3 ESV).

Third, APPROACH YOUR BIBLE READING AS A WORSHIPFUL EXPERIENCE. It becomes important to have a proper attitude and have the right frame of mind and heart as you read the Word. We should approach the Word of God in worship, with a respectful attitude, and a submissive and yielding attitude. We should approach God's Word in awe.

"All these things my hand has made,
  and so all these things came to be,
declares the LORD.
But this is the one to whom I will look:
  he who is humble and contrite in spirit
  and trembles at my word" (Isaiah 66:2 ESV).

Fourth, consider it an AMAZING PRIVILEGE TO READ AND STUDY THE WORD. The Bible was not always available to the common man for many centuries. The Bible was eventually translated and circulated in many of the world languages. Today, we have a priceless gift in your hands. You can read the Word of God and understand the Word by yourself. We have it available in print, in digital form, from our phone apps to our computers. Since it is a privilege to have and to read it, we must consider the Word a great responsibility.

Fifth, develop a REAL INTEREST AS YOU READ A PORTION OF SCRIPTURE. Many times we find reading the Word is dry and boring. We need to develop and foster a real interest in reading. We need to ask ourselves questions when we read certain passages. If you are reading a passage ask yourself "Why did Peter deny Jesus?" "Why did the Pharisees react so viciously against Jesus when He talked about His relationship with His father?" Take notice of the words and the vocabulary, find a connection between sentences, and discover the meaning in each book and chapter. Arouse your curiosity, peak your interest, and you will find joy in reading and studying God's Word.

Sixth, ask the Lord to give you REAL AND TRUE JOY AS YOU READ THE BIBLE. One of the fruits of the Spirit is joy. When you pick up the Word ask God to open up your heart and bring joy to your heart as you open up your heart and yourself to His divine Word.

"But the fruit of the Spirit is love, joy, peace, patience, kindness, goodness, faithfulness" (Galatians 5:22 ESV).

Seventh, search out a TIME AND QUIET PLACE TO SPEND QUALITY TIME READING THE WORD. Most people get distracted if the TV is on or the radio or any other background noise. So if you can find a quiet place to read then we have to learn not to allow things to interfere with our time of reading and studying. We need to also avoid conversations while reading. If we can be undisturbed then we can think through the text as we read the Word. Find a time when you can be alone and a time when you are most awake and alert. For some of you, this may be at 4 or 5 am and for others it might be late at night.

Eighth, BEGIN YOUR TIME IN THE BIBLE WITH PRAYER. One thing we need to learn to do is to pray before we begin to read verses or chapters for the day. We need to pause and ask God to give us clarity of thought when we read, and to show us and convict us when we read the inspired Word. Don't rely on your reading ability; instead depend on God to enlighten you as you prayerfully read.

"Open my eyes, that I may behold wondrous things out of your law" (Psalms 119:18 ESV).

Ninth, read to BENEFIT SPIRITUALLY AND TO FIND GOD'S WILL.

The Bible was written for our instruction, perseverance, and encouragement so that we could have hope. The Bible also warns us and all scripture is profitable for us, teaches us, gives us reproof, correction, and training in righteousness. The Bible also gives us wisdom. The Word also nourishes us and helps us to grow. When you read the Word and seek to find His will while reading and you seek to find the spiritual benefits, you can develop an unquenchable appetite for the Word.

There are times when we all go through periods in our life when reading the Bible becomes a DUTY instead of a DELIGHT. If we use the points listed above we can find a fresh interest and passion for reading and studying the Word of God.

A.W. Tozer said, "The Bible is not an end in itself, but a means to bring men to an intimate and satisfying knowledge of God, that they may enter into Him, that they may delight in His presence, may taste and know the inner sweetness of the very God Himself in the core and center of their hearts." 64

"For whatever was written in former days was written for our instruction, that through endurance and through the encouragement of the Scriptures we might have hope" (Romans 15:4 ESV).

"Now these things happened to them as an example, but they were written down for our instruction, on whom the end of the ages has come" (1 Corinthians 10:11 ESV).

"All Scripture is God-breathed and is useful for teaching, rebuking, correcting and training in righteousness, so that the servant of God[a] may be thoroughly equipped for every good work" (2 Timothy 3:16-17 NIV).

"If you point these things out to the brothers and sisters, you will be a good minister of Christ Jesus, nourished on the truths of the faith and of the good teaching that you have followed" (1 Timothy 4:6 NIV).

UNDERSTANDING

So if you believe the Word of God is truth and you believe the Bible is really the Word of God and if you believe the Bible contains the truth about how we should live and conduct our lives then are those beliefs reflected in your daily life? The psalmist prayed for understanding so that he might live. When we read we need to pray for understanding so we can follow God and obey what He says in His Word.

In my last book "Both Sides of the Coin", I used an illustration that Chuck Swindoll had used in one of his books. I do not want to repeat that illustration here, but I will word it in a different way.

Let's say I own a business and you and some friends have been hired to work for me. Everything is going really well and the company is growing. I decide to go on a long trip for a year and so I ask you and all the others to take care of things while I am gone. During that one year, I write many letters expressing my concerns and desires for the company. Finally, when I return, I walk up to the front of the building and I notice the weeds in the flower beds, the front windows are broken, I hear loud music coming from within the building. I go inside and the receptionist is sleeping, I walk past the offices and there are people missing, and there are others in different offices playing on their computers, and horseplay in another office. I call everyone together because I notice the company has lost money instead of making money. I ask, "What has happened? Didn't you get my letters?" You reply, "Oh, yeah, we did. We got all of your letters. We've even made a book out of them and we have memorized some of them, but not many. In fact, we have a 'letter study' every week. You know, those were really great letters." I then ask, "But what did you do about my instructions?" You all respond, "Do? Well, nothing. But we read every letter."

Now that story may sound crazy to you, but in reality, this is the way most Christians are living. We read the Word occasionally, we hear the Word at church, we go there every week, and study the letters of God, but we do nothing about it. The psalmist wants to understand as he studies the Word so that he can live, so he can obey. We need to pray for understanding, but while we are praying we must have intentions on living out the Words we read. We covered some of this in earlier chapters, we can't just pick and choose what we want to obey we must obey the whole Word.

We must LISTEN as we read, we must LEARN as we read, and we must LIVE what we read. When we are listening we must be ready and willing to obey the Word of God. When we learn the Word we must obey. Some have said that it only takes 21 days to form a habit. If you can change your habits you will be able to change the way you live. We must live out the Word by changing the way we live. All of this starts with a willing heart and openness to hear God speak through His divine Word. Billy Graham once said**, "God does not call us to be successful, but to be obedient."**

SONG FROM THE HEART

The song the psalmist is singing in these eight verses is a song that we need to sing. He says he has a passion for the Word of God because his enemies have ignored the Word. When others are not following the Word, we need not get mad and upset at them we should pray for them, we should cry for them, but we should also be even more passionate for our God and for His Word.

"A man goes to the doctor and says, "Doctor, I'm coughing my heart out. It feels like my lungs are burning up." "Let's take a look," says the doctor. So the doctor examines him. "It's not looking good. But you're in luck. I've got a bottle of medicine here. The instructions are on the bottle. It'll clear this up in three days." Five days later the man returns. "Doctor, you told me this stuff would cure me in three days. I'm not getting better. I'm getting worse." "Did you read the instructions?" the doctor asks. "Of course, I read the instructions," the man replies. "It says..." The doctor snatches the bottle out of his hand. "Gimme that bottle. This bottle is unopened." "Listen, you came in

to see me. I examined you. I diagnosed your problem. I gave you the medicine. Now it's up to you." How many Christians know that God's Word has the power to transform their lives, to heal, to deliver, to give wisdom, to counsel, but they just never seem to get around to reading it on a regular basis?" [65]

"If you could buy a cure-all pill that was guaranteed to heal any sickness, how valuable would it be to you? Wouldn't you guard it? Keep it close? Think of it as very precious? God's Word has solutions to all mankind's ills, and yet sometimes Christians don't even read it." [66]

OUR PRAYER

Heavenly Father, help us to have a passion for Your Word and for You. As we read Your Word, give us understanding. Help us to live by Your Word so that we may bring honor and we will glorify your name. In Jesus Name, Amen.

Song #19

"Sleepless Tonight"

"It's one of those sleepless nights with a lot of thoughts going through my mind." **67**
Unknown

Psalms 119:145-152

145 "*I cried with my whole heart; hear me, O LORD: I will keep thy statutes.*

146 *I cried unto thee; save me, and I shall keep thy testimonies.*

147 *I prevented the dawning of the morning, and cried: I hoped in thy word.*

148 *Mine eyes prevent the night watches, that I might meditate in thy word.*

149 *Hear my voice according unto thy lovingkindness: O LORD, quicken me according to thy judgment.*

150 *They draw nigh that follow after mischief: they are far from thy law.*

151 *Thou art near, O LORD; and all thy commandments are truth.*

152 Concerning thy testimonies, I have known of old that thou hast founded them forever."

Once again in these eight verses, we see the psalmist falls into deep despair. He is desperate and he cries out with all of his heart. "Answer me!" "Save me!" He gets up early in the morning to pray and yet he gets very little sleep because he stays awake in his bed meditating on God's Word. His oppressors are closing in on him and are getting closer, but he knows that he is to rely on God. Have you ever been desperate, really desperate to hear from God? What did you do to reach out to God? We will examine these eight verses to see what the psalmist did and see what we need to do in times of desperation.

The 19th letter of the Hebrew alphabet is **QOPH**. The root verb *qwp* covers a circular motion and that it also serves to denote the ear of an ax or needle or the back of the head. Some also believe it is used as a compass or to go around.

Vs. 145-I call with
>ALL my heart
>ANSWER me, Lord, I will do as you
>ASK.

Vs. 146-I call out
>SAVE me, I will keep Your
>STATUTES.

Vs. 147-I'm up before sunrise to call for Your
>HELP, I put my
>HOPE in Your Word.

Vs. 148-I stay awake all night
>PRAYING and meditating on Your
>PROMISES.

Vs. 149-Hear my voice in
>ACCORDANCE with Your love,
>ALWAYS preserve my life
>ACCORDING to Your Word.

Vs. 150-Those who are out to get me
>COME even
>CLOSER, but they go
>FARTHER
>FROM Your truth.

Vs. 151-YOU are closest to me, God
    YOUR Word is truth.

Vs. 152-LONG ago I
    LEARNED from Your Word, and it will
    LAST forever.

SLEEPLESS NIGHTS

The psalmist has probably had a lot of sleepless nights, and if you are like me, you probably have many as well. They can be very frustrating and they can make a sane person go crazy. Maybe you are worried, afraid, physically sick, restless, troubled, or stressed. Whatever the reason, I am sure you have experienced the tossing and the turning of another sleepless night. Maybe it's one of those nights where you throw the blankets off, flip your pillow over a dozen times, check the time every 5 minutes, get up and turn on the TV and surf the channels not finding anything to watch, and then you get up and look out the window to see if your neighbors are awake. All of us have a sleepless night now and then.

There have been many studies concerning people and their sleep. The studies have shown that 62% of Americans have trouble sleeping one or more nights a week. There are around 40 million Americans who suffer from a chronic sleep disorder. There are 70 million Americans who suffer from insomnia. There are 18 million Americans who suffer from sleep apnea. The studies have also shown that 49.2 million Americans have trouble sleeping because they are concentrating on other things. 38.8 million are remembering things, 28.2 million are working on their hobbies, 22.3 million are taking care of financial needs. [68]

Another reason why many believe that Psalms 119 is written by King David is because he had many sleepless nights when he was on the run from family and from Saul. Sometimes our SLEEPLESS night can turn into a STRESSFUL day. King David trusted God and went to sleep knowing the Lord would keep him through the night. The psalmist has realized the same thing, for in verse 147 of chapter 119, he says, "I have put my hope in Your Word."

Charles Spurgeon said, *"It is the most bitter of all afflictions to be led to fear that there is no help for us in God."*[69] Those are times when we feel crushed, we feel as if the floor has been pulled out from under us and we feel that someone has put grease on the rope we are holding on to.

King David was running again, and he was in danger because his son Absalom was after him. Psalms 3 is the psalm that David wrote while fleeing from his own son. Let's take a look at the psalm and see if we sometimes fall into the same scenario.

First, he expressed his great CRISIS. He was experiencing deep anxious feelings and his enemies have risen up against him.

"O LORD, how many are my foes! Many are rising against me; many are saying of my soul, there is no salvation for him in God. Selah" (Psalms 3:1-2 ESV).

Sometimes we feel like our enemies are all against us and we feel like we are small and we will be crushed. We feel insignificant at times in our lives, and think the whole world is against us. As already stated, David was fleeing from his son. His son has been living in rebellion. Are you living with a son, daughter or a spouse who has turned their lives against you because of what you believe and the commitment you have made for God? Are you facing an uphill battle in pursuing God and His goals for your life? Maybe you feel like the environment where you work is a battle and instead of swords, knives, and bullets, it is rumors, lies, gossip, deceit and misrepresentation against you. When you go to work you dread the jungle at the office. Maybe there is that one person or animal that is pushing your buttons trying to find that vulnerable spot. You hear them saying, "God will not deliver you." We all at times feel the assault of the enemy.

Second, he is CONFIDENT in the Lord. He is trusting in God knowing that He is his shield. He knows that he will have the victory. He takes his mind off of his enemies and focuses all his attention on the only one that can give him victory. *"But you, O LORD, are a shield about me, my glory, and the lifter of my head. I cried aloud to the LORD, and he answered me from his holy hill. Selah" (Psalms 3:4-5 ESV).*

Like a mark in a score of music we see the crescendo in David's song here. He pauses for a moment and cries aloud to God and is essentially saying "Praise the Lord", You are my shield, you are the "lifter of my head." David realizing God is the one who can lift his head when his head is been held low. There are times when we look at the problems we face and we see all of our weakness and it all seems impossible. When we bring God into the picture we will see Him in His true greatness. The mountains that seem so big become small hills. The giants that are larger than life become like grasshoppers. The fears we have become occasions to see the great hand of God in our lives.

Third, David CRIES out to God and he knows that God hears his cry. He was leaning on the Lord and he says, *"I lay down and slept; I woke again, for the LORD sustained me. I will not be afraid of many thousands of people who have set themselves against me all around" (Psalms 3:5-6 ESV).*

We have to be willing to hand our problems over to the Lord. We should be willing to say, "Lord, You are bigger than this problem, and nothing gets out of hand with You." David prayed, *"Arise, O Lord! Save me, O my God! For you strike all my enemies on the cheek; you break the teeth of the wicked. Salvation belongs to the Lord; your blessing be on your people! Selah" (Psalms 3:7-8 ESV).*

When we hand our problems, worries, restlessness, troubles, sicknesses, fears and stresses over to the Lord then we can be like David and go to sleep knowing the Lord will deliver you.

MEDITATION

The psalmist stayed awake and had a sleepless night and because of this, he meditated on God's Word. We need to learn how to meditate on the Word of God. One of the most neglected things in the Christian life is that of meditation. Now I am not talking meditation where you sit with your legs crossed on a mat, putting your thumb and finger together while chanting some Gregorian chant. I am talking about meditating on God's Word, which is actually commanded by our Lord throughout scripture. Very few Christians have been taught how important it is to pay close attention to what they think about. Either I read this or hear this somewhere:

"Watch your thoughts; they become your words.
Watch your words; they become your actions.
Watch your actions; they become your habits.
Watch your habits; they become your character.
Watch your character; it becomes your destiny."

Let's pause and think for a moment about our daily life and see if we can pinpoint some areas where we need to work. When we think about certain things and we don't focus on God or take the time to meditate on His Word or we don't take those things to Him we can become bogged down in our own thinking and eventually if we don't get that thinking pattern taken care of it will shape us and our destiny.

Think about these things for a moment. How much time do we spend worrying about this or that?

 How much time do we spend grumbling and complaining and we feel sorry for ourselves?

How much time do we spend thinking about the TV shows we watch?

How much time do we re-live the bad things people do to us?

Do we keep a record in our heads of all of our misfortunes?

Do we allow ourselves to be angry for long periods of time?

Do we think about getting revenge on those who have hurt us?

Do we think about all the bad things that might happen to us?

How much time do we actually meditate on the Word of God when we read it?

What are we meditating on? Whatever you are thinking about in your heart is what you are meditating on. The things that we allow in our hearts to dwell on are the things that we are building our lives on for the future. Your inner life is an accurate picture and representation of the real you. No matter what service you perform for God, or what you appear to be to others, the important thing is your inner self. Look what Jesus Christ told the Pharisees.

"Woe to you, scribes and Pharisees, hypocrites! For you clean the outside of the cup and the plate, but inside they are full of greed and self-indulgence. You blind Pharisee! First clean the inside of the cup and the plate, that the outside also may be clean.

"Woe to you, scribes and Pharisees, hypocrites! For you are like whitewashed tombs, which outwardly appear beautiful, but within are full of dead people's bones and all uncleanness. [28] So you also outwardly appear righteous to others, but within you are full of hypocrisy and lawlessness" (Matthew 23:25-28 ESV).

The Pharisees were hypocritical they spent all of their time making sure they obeyed the letter of the law perfectly. It looked like from the outside, they were keeping God's law perfectly and, therefore, they were righteous men. In spite of all their work, they are all dismissed as being filled with greed, self-indulgent, hypocritical, and wicked. God was not impressed with them. God is not impressed with what we appear to be. Many

Christians are good at "playing church". God is interested in what we are like on the inside. His goal is to clean us from the inside out.

This brings us to the point of meditation. If we are going to change on the inside, we need to learn how to meditate on God's Word. Let's take a look at the word meditation. It means to "contemplate or reflect, to focus our thoughts on something, to ponder over, or to plan a project in the mind."

When we meditate we are using our minds and our hearts. We think about things every day and whether we realize it or not, we all spend a big portion of our time in some kind of meditation. There are many times we meditate on the things that do not help us grow at all. Often the things we meditate on are simply sinful. Our meditation should be pleasing to the Lord.

"May my meditation be pleasing to him,
  as I rejoice in the LORD" (Psalms 104:34 NIV).

If we want our meditation to please the Lord, and we know that we should meditate on the Word of God, then what is the best way for us to accomplish this?

First we must PRAYERFULLY MEDITATE. When we read the Bible we are not just reading a book, we are reading the sacred, holy and divine Word of God. The words printed therein are the words God has given to us so we might know Him, love Him, and obey Him. So when we enter into the time of our Bible reading and study we must do it bathed in prayer. We should prayerfully ask God to open our eyes so we can understand and apply the truth of God to our lives. If we don't prayerfully meditate, our times of reading and study will be dry, listless, and fruitless.

Second we must PEACEFULLY MEDITATE. We should find a quiet place. It is very difficult for most of us to give deep, concentrated thought to a passage of scripture if we are surrounded with distractions. Effective meditation occurs when we cut out those distractions. If you are trying to study the Word of God in the middle of Starbuck's or some kind of coffee shop, it will probably be to your disadvantage. If you are trying to study with the television tuned into your favorite show, you might not find the full potential of your study. I have mentioned some of these things in the previous chapter, but some find it easier to get up a little early to study, or like me, I find it easier at night when everyone else has gone to bed. Effective meditation on God's Word usually happens in the stillness of the morning or night.

Third we must PUT INTO WORDS OUR MEDITATION. We must practice on being vocal. Just because you are in a quiet setting doesn't mean you have to be quiet. God speaks to us when we read scripture and sometimes it is appropriate to respond vocally to God's promptings. Now I am not saying you have to "shout" it out because your family might not like that if it is early morning or late night. The Bible is the living Word of God and sometimes we must interact with scripture, responding to its commands, rejoicing in its promises and delighting in its revelations. We need to stop treating the Word of God like some dry textbook. Sometimes it calls for an out loud response to God by rejoicing, prayer, and thanksgiving.

Fourth we must have a PEN IN HAND WHEN MEDITATING. If we would practice carrying a pen and paper into our study time then we will actually remember more of what we study if we write things down. I have never really had a problem with this because in college we were always encouraged to take notes when a preacher or pastor spoke, we took notes in class, and when we had our own private devotional time. When we write things down it can have a transforming effect on our devotional and study time. If you will write things down when you study it will force you to think through the passages and the verses. It will also help you to fight off distractions. It will help you focus all of your attention to the words that are in front of you. One of the things that some people do is to get a notebook and keep a journal of what they write down. I have always made it a practice to write down notes when I am in a church service this also aids me in my own study. John Piper put it this way, *"A pastor will not be able to feed his flock rich and challenging insight into God's word unless he becomes a disciplined thinker. But almost none of us do this by nature. We must train ourselves to do it. And one of the best ways to train ourselves to think about what we read is to read with a pen in hand and to write down a train of thought that comes to mind. Without this, we simply cannot sustain a sequence of questions and answers long enough to come to penetrating conclusions"*

SONG FROM THE HEART

We have clearly seen what the psalmist was singing here and we see he is in great despair but he knows to trust and meditate on God's Word. He says that he had a sleepless night because he was meditating on God's Word and promises.

"My eyes stay open through the watches of the night, that I may meditate on your promises."

God's Word is powerful and it is the same today as it was before the world was created. God's Word is the same today as it will be long after this world has passed away. At the end of these eight verses, the psalmist tells us that God's Word will endure and last forever. God character doesn't change and His view on how humans should live their lives doesn't change. God's judgment of right and wrong doesn't change. He is the same and His Word is the same.

"It is gratitude that prompted an old man to visit an old broken pier on the eastern seacoast of Florida. Every Friday night, until his death in 1973, he would return,

walking slowly and slightly stooped with a large bucket of shrimp. The seagulls would flock to this old man, and he would feed them from his bucket. Many years before, in October 1942, Captain Eddie Rickenbacker was on a mission in a B-17 to deliver an important message to General Douglas MacArthur in New Guinea. But there was an unexpected detour which would hurl Captain Eddie into the most harrowing adventure of his life.

Somewhere over the South Pacific, the Flying Fortress became lost beyond the reach of radio. Fuel ran dangerously low, so the men ditched their plane in the ocean. For nearly a month Captain Eddie and his companions would fight the water, and the weather, and the scorching sun. They spent many sleepless nights recoiling as giant sharks rammed their rafts. The largest raft was nine by five. The biggest shark...ten feet long. But of all their enemies at sea, one proved most formidable: starvation. Eight days out, their rations were long gone or destroyed by the salt water. It would take a miracle to sustain them. And a miracle occurred.

In Captain Eddie's own words, "Cherry," that was the B-17 pilot, Captain William Cherry, "read the service that afternoon, and we finished with a prayer for deliverance and a hymn of praise. There was some talk, but it tapered off in the oppressive heat. With my hat pulled down over my eyes to keep out some of the glare, I dozed off."

Now this is still Captain Rickenbacker

talking..."Something landed on my head. I knew that it was a seagull. I don't know how I knew, I just knew. Everyone else knew too. No one said a word, but peering out from under my hat brim without moving my head, I could see the expression on their faces. They were staring at that gull. The gull meant food...if I could catch it."

And the rest, as they say, is history. Captain Eddie caught the gull. Its flesh was eaten. Its intestines were used for bait to catch fish. The survivors were sustained and their hopes renewed because a lone seagull, uncharacteristically hundreds of miles from land, offered itself as a sacrifice. You know that Captain Eddie made it.

And now you also know...that he never forgot. Because every Friday evening, about sunset...on a lonely stretch along the eastern Florida seacoast...you could see an old man walking...white-haired, bushy-eye browed, slightly bent. His bucket filled with shrimp was to feed the gulls...to remember that one which, on a day long past gave itself without a struggle...like manna in the wilderness." **70**

OUR PRAYER

Heavenly Father, today we bring our greatest needs to You. Help me to sleep well and not worry, stress, or be fearful, but know that we can trust in You. Thanks for hearing our prayers, and may we continually meditate on Your Word. We ask You to sustain us when troubles are around us. In Jesus Name, Amen.

Song #20

"It All Adds Up"

"The Truth is not a religion, the correct
denomination, the teachings of some great man
or woman, a body of knowledge, the "right"
book, a deep philosophy, the correct concept or
a set of laws or governing principles. It can never
be ascertained through the "scientific method,"
logic or reasoning. All these are instruments that
fall far short of being able to fathom "the Truth."[71]
Gary Amirault

Psalms 119:153-160

[153] *"Consider mine affliction, and deliver me:
for I do not forget thy law.*

[154] *Plead my cause, and deliver me: quicken me
according to thy word.*

[155] *Salvation is far from the wicked: for they
seek not thy statutes.*

[156] *Great are thy tender mercies, OLORD:
quicken me according to thy judgments.*

[157] *Many are my persecutors and mine enemies;
yet do I not decline from thy testimonies.*

158 I beheld the transgressors, and was grieved; because they kept not thy word.

159 Consider how I love thy precepts: quicken me, O LORD, according to thy lovingkindness.

160 Thy word is true from the beginning: and every one of thy righteous judgments endureth forever."

Once again, as we enter these verses, we see the psalmist is still living in a state of desperation. He turns his eyes to his oppression, but there seems to be a difference in his requests of God this time. Three times in these eight verses he prays "preserve my life." The Hebrew word literally translates to "revive." The psalmist asks God for deliverance from his affliction and redemption from his situation and his life to be revived. Why does the psalmist ask these things? So that he will continue to keep God's Word that he may experience God's mercies and that he may enjoy the benefits of God's love.

We are at the 20th letter in the Hebrew alphabet and it is **RESH**. The very common word *rosh* basically means head, but is used to indicate whatever leads or comes first: captain, summit, cap stone. Preceded by the particle *beth* and in the form *reshit* first, beginning, best, it is the first word of the Bible: *Breshit*, meaning In the beginning. The third usage of this word is *resh*, means poverty, from the root rush meaning to be poor.

Vs. 153-Deliver me from my sufferings and
　　　HELP me, for I
　　　HAVE not forgotten Your Word.

Vs. 154-Defend my cause and
　　　REDEEM me,
　　　REVIVE me according to Your Word.

Vs. 155-SALVATION is far from the
　　　WICKED. They do not
　　　SEEK out Your
　　　WORD.

Vs. 156-Your
　　　LOVE is great
　　　LORD. Revive my
　　　LIFE according to Your
　　　LAWS.

Vs. 157-Many are
>THOSE who persecute me, I have not
>TURNED from Your Word.

Vs. 158-I
>LOOK on the quitters with
>LOATHING. They
>WALK away from Your
>WORD.

Vs. 159-See how I
>LOVE Your Word. Revive my
>LIFE,
>LORD in accordance with Your
>LOVE.

Vs. 160-Your Words
>ALL
>ADD up to TRUTH.
>ALL Your righteous Words
>ARE forever.

THE ATTORNEY

The phrase "Plead my cause" or "Defend my cause" in verse 154 is a legal term. The psalmist is asking God to be his advocate, he is asking God to represent him as his attorney. As followers of Christ, we have the promise of a divine attorney that will represent us in God's courtroom. Our attorney is Jesus Christ. He is our advocate.

My dear children, I write this to you so that you will not sin. But if anybody does sin, we have an advocate with the Father—Jesus Christ, the Righteous One. He is the atoning sacrifice for our sins, and not only for ours but also for the sins of the whole world" (1 John 2:1-2 NIV).

Now over the years, there have been numerous jokes about attorneys. But, an attorney, when you need one is a very important professional who has been given a certain amount of authority and power. Lawyers practice law. The psalmist asks God to "defend his cause." In the book of Lamentations, Jeremiah uses the same terminology by saying "You took my case, You redeemed my life."

"You, Lord, took up my case; you redeemed my life. LORD, you have seen the wrong done to me. Uphold my cause" (Lamentations 3:58-59 NIV)!

In the book of Lamentations, the prophet Jeremiah laments the destruction of Jerusalem and the spiritual condition of what is of Israel.

Jeremiah like the psalmist is at the point of desperation because of his oppressors. Fear becomes a factor and the prophet Jeremiah weeps uncontrollably. In verses 52 through 54 of Lamentations 3, the prophet speaks of his enemies and how he has been hunted down without cause.

"Those who were my enemies without cause hunted me like a bird. They tried to end my life in a pit and threw stones at me; the waters closed over my head, and I thought I was about to perish" (Lamentations 3:52-54 NIV).

Have you ever had a similar experience? Have you ever felt like Jeremiah did? Have you ever felt like the psalmist?

God sometimes seems far away, and it seems that nothing is going right, our life is a mess, and we are being pursued by people who are not friendly! And we are miserable! But God hears Jeremiah, and he hears us!

If you will notice in the passage where the psalmist writes and in the passage where Jeremiah writes, they ask God to be their lawyer but they also want God to redeem them. There is a link with those two phrases. In the Old Testament, there is a person known as the "kinsman-redeemer. In the book of Leviticus we see that if any of the Israelites relatives go bankrupt and are forced to sell some land then a close relative can buy it back for them, he is known as the "kinsman-redeemer."

Another popular kinsman-redeemer was Boaz in the book of Ruth where he made it possible for Ruth and Naomi to survive by allowing Ruth to pick grain from his fields.

Notice in Leviticus the text speaks of "bankruptcy." Who do people call when bankruptcy becomes the only option when dealing with finances? It is an unfortunate option and a scary one. We call a lawyer, one that practices in bankruptcy. A lawyer that deals in bankruptcy know all there is to know about bankruptcy, what forms to file, and the process one must go through when filing for bankruptcy. What the Bible is saying here is that it is not an attorney or a lawyer that is helping us to get out of a financial situation but we need a kinsman-redeemer. This redeemer is the one who will buy back the land and keep it in the family. The purpose of what we see in the Old Testament is more a covenant or a contract more than a legal code. This was designed to help the people of Israel to truly become the people of God. Jeremiah cries out to the Lord and says, "Lord, You are my lawyer! Plead my case!" He is seeking not to right a legal wrong, but to be redeemed by God and his situation, and that of Israel to be set straight. The Lord would redeem Jeremiah and Israel, He would act as their attorney, their lawyer, and He would free them, politically and spiritually from the bondage of exile and sin so that when Jesus came to earth and hung on the cross for their sin, He came to a people who had been redeemed time and time again through the Law but would soon be once and for all redeemed by His sacrifice on their behalf, and ours as well.

I don't know of any attorney who would be willing to take the punishment for a client. A lawyer will represent and advise his client, but he doesn't go to jail for them. Jesus Christ is more than an attorney He is also our redeemer and our Savior.

REVIVE ME

I mentioned it earlier in this chapter, but three times the psalmist says, "revive me." When you take a closer look he words it three different ways. First he says, "Revive me according to Your Word." Second he says, "Revive me according to Your laws." Third he says, "Revive me according to Your love."

There are times when we all need "revival"; we need to be renewed, revitalized, reinvigorated, and rescued. The question I would ask for myself and for you is, "Where will you turn for revival?

We should turn to the Lord, for He is the only source of a true spiritual revival. Let's look at the three differences and see why the psalmist put it in three distinct ways.

First the writer asked the Lord to revive him ACCORDING TO THE WORD. The psalmist calls on God to deliver him because he has suffered in his circumstances. He takes his relationship with God seriously and he brings his case before God. He knows that he has been obedient to God's Word and so he knows that God uses the Word to

351

deliver him to revive him in his difficult circumstances. When we are in dire circumstances be assured we can go to God's Word for renewal, for a revival. We have mentioned it all the way through this book and it is mentioned all the way through Psalms 119, we must constantly rely on God's Word.

Second the writer asked the Lord to revive him ACCORDING TO HIS LAWS. Knowing that his enemies have not sought out God's laws, the psalmist has distanced himself from the wicked. He has been faithful before God and so he doesn't ask for God to answer because of his own merit but because of God's mercies. His oppressors are those who actually attack him and secretly despise him. They do not have any influence on him because he refuses to turn aside from God's Word. It is the very Word of God that has given him a true knowledge of God. The psalmist continues by telling us he actually "loathes" his enemies because they do not keep the Word of God. He knows the Lord has great compassion and, therefore, he knows that he can be revived through the law of God.

Third, the psalmist asked God to revive him ACCORDING TO HIS LOVE. The psalmist wants to live out the Word of God. Notice in this his final asking for God to renew him or revive him he has confidence in knowing that God loves him and he was asking this time based upon God's loving-kindness. He also based his request upon the fact that he loved God's Word. The first two times he based his request upon the fact that he had been obedient to God's Word. He knows that God is faithful and God is working in his life. God is working anew in our lives every day, by His grace. Matter of fact it is usually in our darkest hours, in our hour of desperation when revival comes.

IT ALL ADDS UP TO TRUTH

The psalmist writes these words when he finishes up this section. He knows that the sum of God's Word is the truth, meaning it can be trusted. Looking at the Word and adding it all up and getting a total, and that total is truth. Not just true, the WORD IS TRUTH. A half-hearted faith and a half-hearted approach to God's Word will never bring revival or a renewal. We must believe the totality of God's Word which is forever true and forever eternal.

When you go to court in the United States and you are going to be a witness you are asked this: "Do you promise to tell the truth, the whole truth and nothing but the truth, so help me God?"

"This is what the LORD says: "Maintain justice and do what is right, for my salvation is close at hand and my righteousness will soon be revealed. Blessed is the one who does this—the person who holds it fast, who keeps the Sabbath without desecrating it, and keeps their hands from doing any evil" (Isaiah 56:1-2 NIV).

I know a few people that deny the Bible is the absolute Word of truth. They do not believe it was written through the inspiration of the Holy Spirit. They pick and choose the parts they believe are truth. The whole Bible is the whole truth. In Isaiah, we read the words "keep justice and do righteousness." Where do these come from? They come from God!!

God is Truth

*"Give ear, O heavens, and I will speak, and
let the earth hear the words of my mouth.
May my teaching drop as the rain, my speech
distill as the dew, like gentle rain upon the
tender grass, and like showers upon the herb.
For I will proclaim the name of the* LORD;
*ascribe greatness to our God" (Deuteronomy
32:1-3 ESV).*

He is the Rock, His work is perfect and all His ways
are just. He is a God of truth and without injustice.
He is righteous and upright.

Jesus is Truth

*"Jesus said to him, "I am the way, and the
truth, and the life. No one comes to the Father
except through me" (John 14:6 ESV).*

Spirit of Truth

*"This is he who came by water and blood—
Jesus Christ; not by the water only but by the
water and the blood. And the Spirit is the one
who testifies, because the Spirit is the truth" (1
John 5:6).*

The Word is Truth

"The sum of your word is truth, and every one of your righteous rules endures forever"
(Psalms 119:160 ESV).

Justice and righteousness come from the truth of God's Word and His character. To be just means to be impartial in action and judgment, to be honest, correct and true. God Word and His character are the highest standards by which anything or anyone can be judged.

We all need to look at the truth of God's Word and allow it to shape us and develop us, so we will see the righteousness of God being revealed in us as we pray for and witness to our friends and family. Hold on to God's Word because it is His truth that endures forever. Hold on to His truth as a great treasure and continue to invest His truth into your life.

SONG FROM THE HEART

The psalmist says, "The sum of Your Word is truth, and every one of Your righteous rules endure forever." When you look at the conclusion of the eight verses in this chapter, you will notice that the psalmist loves the Word, believes the Word and always uses the Word.

"In the Supreme Court case between Humanity and Satan, proceedings took on a surprising turn, in the court room when Judge God read out the charge against the defendant (humanity).

Sin was the main charge with a list of violations being read out, some minor & seemingly insignificant while others were major and grotesque. The plaintiff sneered and was getting ready for his closing statement of damnation and requesting for the death penalty. One last witness requested to take the stand to state His witness.
It was then that the Judge gasped and humanity looked surprised. Jesus took the stand and after being sworn in, to tell the Truth, the whole Truth and nothing but the Truth, He requested of Judge God to please take the place and any punishment that might be assigned to humanity as a result of the crime that was committed.

Everyone sighed, humanity cried in disbelief and the plaintiff lost his grin and became angry. After the Judge had a look at Articles 9 of Hebrews, subsection 12 to 28, He accepted the life of Jesus in the place of humanity and what followed was the harshest sentence that was ever laid down on anyone: as the Judge read out the punishment for the crime all became quiet... The Death penalty was imposed on the criminal. No mitigating circumstances were offered or accepted. No mercy was forthcoming. He accepted His fate. He smiled. Love permeated from Him, the peace in the courtroom was beyond words yet the anger of the Judge was unspeakable, He turned away and would not look at the criminal being led away.

He was led away to Calvary where He would be executed with the other criminals.

The plaintiff smiled and waited for applause yet no congratulations were given. Humanity was free.

Justice had been served, Jesus took humanity's place and the price has been paid by His precious blood once for all." [72]

OUR PRAYER

Heavenly Father, we seek Your help today and we ask You to revive us, renew us, reinvigorate us according to Your Word and love. We know God is our kinsman-redeemer and attorney and we know and thank You that You are the absolute truth. In Jesus Name, Amen.

Song #21

"Nothing Can Make Me Stumble"

"The life of inner peace,
being harmonious and without stress,
is the easiest type of existence."[73]
Norman Vincent Peale

Psalms 119:161-168

[161] *"Princes have persecuted me without a cause: but my heart standeth in awe of thy word.*

[162] *I rejoice at thy word, as one that findeth great spoil.*

[163] *I hate and abhor lying: but thy law do I love.*

[164] *Seven times a day do I praise thee because of thy righteous judgments.*

[165] *Great peace have they which love thy law: and nothing shall offend them.*

[166] *LORD, I have hoped for thy salvation, and done thy commandments.*

¹⁶⁷ My soul hath kept thy testimonies; and I love them exceedingly.

¹⁶⁸ I have kept thy precepts and thy testimonies: for all my ways are before thee."

Resilient, steadfast, and determination are the marks of the writer of Psalms 119. He has lived in despair and he has been faithful in his rejoicing of God's Word. In previous chapters of this book the psalmist has referred to his oppressors, in general, but in this passage, he is more specific. Powerful men, princes, are oppressing him without cause. Even though people in authority are making his life miserable, the writer is resolved to stand in awe of God, rejoice in God's Word, love God's Word, praise God and keep God's commands. The writer in these next eight verses dwells on rejoicing and praising God. He even mentions that he praises God seven times a day. He also tells us that those who love the Word of God will have "great peace" and nothing will make them stumble.

The 21st Hebrew letter is **SIN** or **SHIN**. A derivation from the verb *shanan*, means to sharpen, the word *shen* means tooth or ivory. Both the verb and the noun are used primarily in a literal sense: the sharpening of swords and arrows, but sometimes figuratively: the sharpening of one's tongue (saying sharp, mean words) or the sharpening of one's mind. The noun is famous for its part in the law of retaliation; a soul for a soul, and eye for an eye, a tooth for a tooth, a hand for a hand, a foot for a foot, a branding for a branding, a stripe for a stripe. The letter thanks its name perhaps to it looking like a row of teeth.

Vs. 161-Rulers and
POLITICIANS
PERSECUTE me without cause, I
STAND in awe at Your Word, they keep me
STEADY.

Vs. 162-I
REJOICE in Your promise, I am
RICH.

Vs. 163-I hate and detest
LIES, but I
LOVE Your
LAW.

Vs. 164-SEVEN times a day, I
    STOP and
    SHOUT praises for Your laws are right.

Vs. 165-Great peace comes to
    THOSE who
    LOVE Your
    LAW.
    THEY do not stumble in the dark.

Vs. 166-I wait
    FOR Your salvation Lord, I
    FOLLOW Your commands.

Vs. 167-I
    GUARD Your Word, I
    GREATLY love it.

Vs. 168-I obey Your
    DIRECTIONS and Your
    DECREES, my life is an open
    BOOK
    BEFORE You.

SEVEN TIMES

When I looked at these eight verses the one that stood out to me the most was verse 164, where the psalmist writes "seven times a day I praise

You." The Bible mentions the word "seven" 735 times. So obviously, the number seven has a significant meaning. So why was seven so important to the Hebrews?

When you take the earth with its four corners, North, South, East, and West and add the number three, which is the number for God being the trinity, God the Father, God the Son, and God the Holy Spirit, you get the total of SEVEN, which stands for the divine COMPLETENESS OF GOD. Here we have seven representing the completeness of the union of heaven and earth.

In the book of Revelation, the word "seven" is used 54 times. The whole Word of God is founded upon the number "seven." Let's take a look at how it is used throughout the Word starting from the beginning of creation. God created the world in six days and on the seventh He rested. We have seven days in a week. This shows completeness or perfection. The word "created" is used seven times in connection with God's creative work.

In music, we have seven notes in the scale, with the eighth note taking us back to "DO" or the first note in the scale. God made the sounds, man named the notes. God made seven days in a week, man named the days.

When Noah entered into the ark, he took seven pairs of clean animals, and after they entered the ark it was seven days before the floods came. Before Aaron and his priestly sons could enter into the tabernacle they had to go through seven days of consecration. On the Day of Atonement, the priest would sprinkle the blood on the mercy seat seven times. All these things show the completeness of God.

When Israel went to take the city of Jericho, they were ordered to march around the city seven times on the seventh day. There were seven feast days of God and they are Passover, Unleavened, First-Fruits, Pentecost, Atonement, Trumpets, and Tabernacle. There were seven branches on the candlestick in the Holy Place; this is a picture of the completeness of God as the light for the souls of man. In the days of Joseph, there were seven years of PLENTY and seven years of FAMINE.

Solomon spent seven years building the Temple and spent seven days keeping the Feast. Job had seven sons. When his friends came to give him advice they spent seven days and seven nights in silence, and afterward they were required to offer seven bullocks and seven rams. Naaman had to wash seven times in the Jordan River.

Jesus Christ told us to forgive someone "Seventy times Seven", meaning we should forgive someone until we are complete. Jesus Christ spoke seven times while He was on the cross. There were seven men of good report chosen to administer alms of the church in the New Testament. Jesus Christ performed seven miracles on the seventh day, the Sabbath.

There are seven dispensations and they are Innocence, Conscience, Government, Patriarchal, Law, Grace, and Millenium. Seven times the "Book of Life" is mentioned in the Bible. In the book of Revelation, we have seven churches, seven seals, seven trumpets, seven personages, seven vials, seven dooms and seven new things. Seven Sevens make up the book of Revelation and it is the completeness of ALL things.

Often times I have been in discussion with an someone who does not believe God created us or the earth. Let's take a look at science and God's creation relating to the number seven.

There have been different kinds of tests performed scientifically on the human body and we have found out that our body changes every seven years. There are seven bones in the neck. There are seven bones in the ankle. We also have seven holes or openings for our head. Human physiology is also marked with seven. Conception to birth for a human child is 280 days which divided by 7 equals 40 weeks.

It is truly amazing and truly wonderful how God formed so many things in the form of seven.

The traveling singer, the writer of Psalms 119 recognizes this as he says he will praise God "seven" times a day. How many times do we praise God in a day? We might praise God one time during the day, maybe more. We might hear a song or a sermon, and praise God, but most of the time we spend our days complaining. Most of the time we spend our days talking with others about sports, shopping, other people, joking, yelling at our kids, and each other. I understand there are times when we have to talk about other things, when we are doing our jobs, in a meeting, having an important phone call, talking about our finances with our spouse, helping kids with their homework, or telling others about Jesus Christ. But how many times in a day do we praise Jesus? Do we praise Him once a day, zero times a day or more than seven?

Here is a suggestion for praising God seven times a day. These are just guidelines.

1. When you first wake up.
2. As you are getting ready for your day.
3. When you leave your house for work.
4. At lunch time.
5. When you are coming home from work.
6. At dinner time.
7. Right before you go to sleep.

The psalmist sang as he traveled, and he kept close to God's Word through his prayer and his praise. Years ago I read this phrase and I still have it written in my Bible. Prayer + Praise = POWER!

GREAT PEACE

The title of this chapter is taken from verse 165 in which the psalmist tells us that we can have "great peace if we love God's law" and "nothing can make us stumble." In a world in which people struggle to find peace, the followers of Jesus Christ have the opportunity to find peace. Not a worldly peace, but God's kind of peace, a peace that comes from being in a right relationship with Jesus Christ. When we resolve ourselves to follow God regardless of the circumstances around us, we have the promise of God's peace. We can find an inner tranquility of spirit that defies our circumstances.

When we hear the word "peace" we don't always grasp it as a positive concept, most of the time we look at the negative aspect of peace. The positive concept of peace is "Hoping you have all the highest good coming your way." The negative concept of peace is "Hoping you don't get into any trouble." The Hebrew word for peace is "shalom." The word "shalom" is peace in the purest sense, meaning "peace unto you." There are some other languages that look at the word peace and in those languages, the positive aspect of peace is always conveyed. The Quechua Indians have a word for peace that literally translates "to sit down in one's heart." Peace to them is opposite of running around in the midst of constant anxieties. The Chol Indians of Mexico use a word for peace that translates "a quiet heart." Once again we see the idea of not running around in chaos.

The biblical concept of peace doesn't focus on the absence of trouble. The word "peace" in the Bible is unrelated to circumstances; peace is the goodness of life that is not touched by what happens on the outside. You can be caught up in some trials of life and still have peace. Where do we find this kind of peace, and how do we attain it? Where do we find the kind of peace that is not just the absence of trouble? Where do we find the kind of peace that cannot be affected by trouble, danger, or sorrow?

"Peace I leave with you; my peace I give you. I do not give to you as the world gives. Do not let your hearts be troubled and do not be afraid" (John 14:27 NIV).

The peace Jesus is speaking of here gives believers a way to remain calm in the worst of circumstances. This kind of peace that God gives, this "great peace" will help us to rejoice in pain and in trial, to sing in the middle of our suffering, to help us overcome the tears of sorrow. This kind of peace is never ruled by our circumstances but instead overrules them.

Another verse that is used quite often when it comes to "peace" is in Philippians.

"And the peace of God, which transcends all understanding, will guard your hearts and your minds in Christ Jesus" (Philippians 4:7 NIV).

So let's take a look at how this verse fits into our daily lives. We will look at how peace falls into three different categories.

First, we should have PEACE WITH ONE ANOTHER. This is not the attitude that most of us use today. Most of us, want to complain, fight and argue for everything we want in life. There are a lot of people that deal with the "ME" syndrome, by having statements such as, "Me first, and everybody else last," and "It's my way, or no way." When we enter the church we find that it is not any different. You know we are all Christians and we all have Jesus in common so we always get along with each other, we never disagree, right? Wrong! We all disagree at times.

Apparently in the book of Philippians, Paul addressed some who were having some trouble agreeing with each other and not living in peace. He even points out a couple of ladies from the congregation. He also brings in a third party to help these two ladies and the rest of the congregation to find "peace with one another."

"I plead with Euodia and I plead with Syntyche to be of the same mind in the Lord. Yes, and I ask you, my true companion, help these women since they have contended at my side in the cause of the gospel, along with Clement and the rest of my co-workers, whose names are in the book of life" (Philippians 4:2-3 NIV).

I am not sure if you have ever been in a church where the members seemed to always be in a disagreement and they can't seem to get along, but I have many times. One of the things that Satan likes to do is to divide the church. If he gets the people in the church to not live in peace then he can cripple the church and it won't be effective in getting out the good news of Jesus Christ. We need to seek to serve God together and be at peace with one another.

Second, we should have PEACE WITHIN. There are days when we feel like we are on top of the world and everything seems to be going our way. But if we are honest there are a lot of times and most days where we don't feel that way at all. There are days when we carry a heavy burden, times when we are worried about someone or something. There are times when we have problems in our life that just don't seem like it is going to go away. We might be having a problem because we feel guilty because of some sin that we have committed.

There are days when we are concerned about our finances. There are days when we are trying to accomplish something and we just can't seem to get it done.

"Rejoice in the Lord always. I will say it again: Rejoice! Let your gentleness be evident to all. The Lord is near. Do not be anxious about anything, but in every situation, by prayer and petition, with thanksgiving, present your requests to God. And the peace of God, which transcends all understanding, will guard your hearts and your minds in Christ Jesus" (Philippians 4:4-7 NIV).

One thing we need to realize is that Paul is not writing these words while sitting in some ivory tower. Sometimes we get the idea that an author, pastor, or teacher has it all together when they are giving us words of wisdom from God's Word. But most of the time these authors, pastors, and teachers are facing the same kind of trials or circumstances you are facing. Paul was in prison and facing trial, and knew that soon he would be executed. He gives us a formula in these verses on how to find "great peace within."

He tells us to "Rejoice, in the Lord", he tells us to not worry about anything but to pray about everything. I have found that this verse is hard for us. Worry is one of the most common sins that a Christian has. Worry is so common to us, that we don't even try to hide it. It becomes a normal, everyday thing in our lives.

We go to church and our mouths say and sing all the great words. We stand and sing "Great is Thy Faithfulness" but we leave worrying about our finances. We stand and sing "What a friend we have in Jesus, all our sins and griefs to bear", yet we worry and we take very little to God in prayer.

Worry weighs us down. Someone said that worry is assuming responsibility that God never intended for us to have. We have to learn to let Him carry our burdens for us. We need to cast ALL our burdens on Him because He cares for us.

God gives us peace! He can give you and me peace in any circumstance that we encounter.

Third, we are to have PEACE WITH GOD. Paul gives us some special verses here and we should take notice and read them often.

"Finally, brothers and sisters, whatever is true, whatever is noble, whatever is right, whatever is pure, whatever is lovely, whatever is admirable—if anything is excellent or praiseworthy—think about such things. Whatever you have learned or received or heard from me, or seen in me—put it into practice. And the God of peace will be with you" (Philippians 4:8-9 NIV).

Paul presents us with 8 filters that we need to pass everything through. Everything we hear and see needs to go through these filters. We are presented with these filters, and if there is something that doesn't pass through these filters, then it is something we don't need in our hearts and minds.

I worked at an oil company for a while and we had some oil that we called "pit oil", this was oil that we dumped in a big pit, excess oil that we used to flush our trucks and lines. The pit oil could be used again, but it had to be run through a filter before we could use it in a blend. We wanted to make sure we got all the impurities out.

Put everything through these 8 filters. If it is not true, then don't welcome it. It if it's not noble, if it's not right, pure or lovely, then we can't let it find a home in our hearts. If we use all these filters we will have peace with God.

"I have said these things to you, that in me you may have peace. In the world you will have tribulation. But take heart; I have overcome the world" (John 16:33 ESV).

Walking around and looking at people in this world, we find that circumstances overrule people and, therefore, they do not have any peace. We find in churches and other places that people cannot agree, and instead of having peace with each other, they bicker and fight and there is a lack of peace. We find most of the time that we are all "anxious" and we "worry" about a lot of different things and we live our lives on a daily basis with no peace. We fill our hearts and minds with things that do not need to be there and we need to run everything through the filter of God's Word and we will find the peace of God will be with us. The psalmist said that we will have "great peace" if we love the Word of God. If we do this, we will not be stumbling around in the dark looking at our circumstances, worrying about our problems and disagreeing with those we come in contact with. If we love the Word of God we will use the filters of true, right, noble, pure, good, lovely and praiseworthy, and place the things in our life through those filters, we won't fall down in the dark. We will have peace.

SONG FROM THE HEART

Praising God seven times a day and finding great peace was the songs that the psalmist proclaimed in these eight verses. Verse 165 is the song from the heart. "Great peace have those who love your Word; nothing can make them stumble." The psalmist was assured of not stumbling around in the dark, not being worried in a world full of no peace because he loved the Word of God, he read, studied, memorized and used it.

"Tracy Lippard was a beauty queen in Virginia a few years ago. Shortly after crowning her successor, she drove 250 miles to seek revenge on her ex-boyfriend for jilting her & marrying another. She took along a 9mm, a hammer, a butcher knife, rubber gloves, some lighter fluid, and matches.

When she arrived at his house & rang the doorbell, it was answered by his new father-in-law. Tracy faked having car trouble, & asked if she could use the telephone. Once inside the house, she took out her hammer & hit the father-in-law on the head. She stunned him but didn't knock him out.

What she didn't realize was that he was an ex-secret service agent. He grabbed her & as they struggled, she pulled the pistol from her purse & tried to shoot him. That's when the mother-in-law joined the fray & the two of them wrestled her to the floor, holding her until the police arrived.

I have a suspicion that Tracy, with that kind of disposition, was probably never in the running for the Miss Congeniality award. When questioned, she said that she was driven to seek revenge because she needed "inner peace." [74]

"About 20 years ago, Time Magazine featured on its cover 5 missionary families & honored them for their many years of devoted service to others. One of those was the J. Russell Morse family, the family that worked on the border of China, Burma & Tibet. J. Russell Morse had been on furlough for a while and then returned to China when the communists were taking the interior of China.

It wasn't long until communist soldiers came to get him, & they said, "Come with us." He asked, "Can I take some clothing & bedding with me?" They said, "No, you won't need anything. We'll take good care of you." But in his memoirs, he later wrote that he knew they weren't telling the truth.

For 18 months he was held in a communist prison, with 15 of those months spent in solitary confinement. His small cell had no window, only a small hole high up to let in a little bit of light & air, & no bed, just filthy straw on the floor. For 15 months he was never able to see or speak to anyone. Just once a day a small panel was opened in the bottom of his cell door & a bowl of food shoved through. He had no Bible, nothing to read. They had even taken away his glasses so that he could barely see.

In his memoirs he later wrote, "The only things that helped me keep my sanity during that period were the Bible verses & hymns I had memorized. And the one verse that kept me going the most was Philippians 4:6: 'Don't be anxious about anything. Pray about everything, & with thanksgiving let your requests be made known unto God.'" He wrote, "If there was ever a time to be anxious, it was when I was in that prison. And if there ever was a time when it was difficult to pray & be thankful, it was then. But I kept repeating those words in my mind over & over again."

When J. Russell Morse came out of the prison, he didn't have to be deprogrammed because God gave him the peace that transcends all understanding." [75]

OUR PRAYER

Heavenly Father, we look for Your peace in our circumstances and in our times of trouble, grant us this peace. Help us to follow you, and praise you in our circumstances whether they are good or bad. We thank you for the promise of peace. In Jesus Name, Amen.

Song #22

"Singing Our Way to Victory"

"The only thing better than singing is more singing"[76]
Ella Fitzgerald

Psalms 119:169-176

[169] *"Let my cry come near before thee, O LORD: give me understanding according to thy word.*

[170] *Let my supplication come before thee: deliver me according to thy word.*

[171] *My lips shall utter praise, when thou hast taught me thy statutes.*

[172] *My tongue shall speak of thy word: for all thy commandments are righteousness.*

[173] *Let thine hand help me; for I have chosen thy precepts.*

[174] *I have longed for thy salvation, O LORD; and thy law is my delight.*

[175] *Let my soul live, and it shall praise thee; and let thy judgments help me.*

176 I have gone astray like a lost sheep; seek thy servant; for I do not forget thy commandments."

When I was younger, I attended training for two weeks every summer, and while there we were taught how to go out and tell children about the Lord Jesus Christ. I remember one of the courses that we all had to take was the course on "How to Live a Victorious Christian Life." I don't remember much of that course today, but throughout my life there were times when I didn't feel victorious, and I didn't live victorious in life. As we have entered into the final stanza or the final eight verses of Psalms 119, and focusing on the title and singing we see the psalmist has had to deal with oppressors and times when he didn't feel victorious. Since Psalms 119 is centered on the Word of God, we once again ask the question, "What is your opinion of the Bible?" Maybe you find it a frustrating book to read. If you do, then don't give up on reading the Bible. Spend time in prayer, as the psalmist did for more understanding and make a pledge to deepen your knowledge of God's Word, by deeper study. I would encourage you to find an easy to read translation, maybe a study Bible with notes to help you and try reading a book like John or Mark in the New Testament. Maybe you find the Bible fascinating to read and want to dig deeper. Then you might consider a reading plan that will take you through the entire Word of God.

The 22nd letter of the Hebrew alphabet is **TAW**. It means to mark, and its verb means scribble or limit. The word *ta'awa* means boundary (that which is marked).

Vs. 169-Let my
> CRY
> COME into Your
> PRESENCE Lord.
> PROVIDE me with understanding.

Vs. 170-May my
> PRAYERS come into Your
> PRESENCE Lord. Deliver me with Your
> PROMISE.

Vs. 171-Let my
    PRAISE
    POUR from my lips. You have
    TAUGHT me
    TRUTH from Your Word.

Vs. 172-My tongue sings and
    RINGS our Your praise, Your Word is
    RIGHT.

Vs. 173-May Your
    HAND be ready to
    HELP me. I have
    CHOSEN Your
    COMMANDMENTS.

Vs. 174-I
    LONG for Your
    SALVATION. Your
    LAWS have given me
    SATISFACTION.

Vs. 175-LET me
    LIVE, so I can praise You. Your
    STATUTES always
    SUSTAIN me.

Vs. 176-I have
>STRAYED like a lost
>SHEEP.
>SEEK Your
>SERVANT. I will always recognize the
>SOUND of Your Word and voice.

SINGING FOR VICTORY

My youngest daughter has always loved to sing. She started singing when she was really young. She continued to sing and in one of her high school years she was voted the best alto in the state. As she grew closer to the Lord, she knew that she wanted to sing for God and to sing songs of worship. I know that when she faces difficult times in life, she turns to singing. Singing is important in our Christian life and I believe when we worship God through singing it plays a big part in living the victorious Christian life. Let's take some time and look at why singing is so important and why it matters.

First, WHEN YOU SING YOU EXECUTE OBEDIENCE. One thing we must understand, singing is not an option in the Word of God it is a commandment. Look at the following two scriptures.

"Let the word of Christ dwell in you richly, teaching and admonishing one another in all wisdom, singing psalms and hymns and spiritual songs, with thankfulness in your hearts to God" (Colossians 3:16 ESV).

"Do not get drunk on wine, which leads to debauchery. Instead, be filled with the Spirit, speaking to one another with psalms, hymns, and songs from the Spirit. Sing and make music from your heart to the Lord, always giving thanks to God the Father for everything, in the name of our Lord Jesus Christ" (Ephesians 5:18-20 NIV).

If you are a follower of Christ, you are not invited to sing, you are commanded to sing. This doesn't mean you have to have a fabulous voice to sing, it just means you have to sing. We are obeying God when we sing. The songs that we should be singing in our act of obedience though are not songs from Beyoncé, Keith Urban, Mariah Carey, or Usher, but songs of worship, singing the psalms, hymns, and spiritual songs.

Second, WHEN YOU SING YOU ENGAGE IN DIGGING DEEPER IN THE WORD. The verse quoted above on the first point says, "Let the Word dwell in you richly." When we let the Word dwell in us richly we live that out by first teaching, and second singing. Since singing is a command there is a promise that comes to us when we obey by singing and that promise is that the Word of God will dwell in us richly. We dig deep roots in the Word of God by singing the psalms, hymns, and spiritual song. Most church services believe that the songs or the special song is a warm-up for the sermon or something that is a fill in for the service. But if you follow Colossians 3:16, it is clearly given to us that singing stands alongside the preaching as one of the great ways that God uses to have His Word dwell richly in each of us.

Singing is one of the best ways to take Theology home with you because it is a 3-4 minute, easy to memorize, deeply biblical summary of the truths of God's Word. Natalie Grant sings a song titled "In Christ Alone", and that song is full of great theology and great truths from God's Word.

Third, WHEN YOU SING YOU ENHANCE OTHERS AND BUILD THEM UP. Your fellow believers are lifted up when you sing. In Ephesians 5, we are to address one another in psalms and hymns and spiritual songs. When we do what the Bible says and we sing together as a church family we are hearing confessions of faith all around us. When we are singing the song "In Christ Alone" with hundreds of others singing, we are hearing hundreds of testimonies of faith all around us.

Also, when we sing, we are helping those who do not believe because they have a chance to hear those hundreds of testimonies and confessions of faith being sung together. When we worship together we become evangelistic together.

Fourth, WHEN YOU SING YOU ERADICATE SIN IN YOUR LIFE. We probably don't connect singing with warfare. In Colossians 3 we are to literally put sin to death by killing it. In the same chapter we are commanded to love to show peace and forgiveness, to teach and to sing, so therefore, we are being taught that our attitudes and our habits will kill or eradicate sin. In Ephesians 5 we are commanded to address one another in singing psalms and spiritual songs which are prefaced by the verse, "make the best of your time because the days are evil." Let's stop and think about singing just for a moment when it comes to war or killing sin. When you are singing and making melody in your heart to the Lord, Satan really hates the stand you are taking. The stance shows your standing with Christ and you are lifting your eyes, heart, mind and voice to heaven with song. It's hard to lie, be greedy, look at something inappropriate, or think bad thoughts about someone while singing to the Lord. A singing heart doesn't easily give in to temptation. A singing heart has the power to overcome evil and eradicate sin.

Fifth, WHEN YOU SING YOU ARE ENERGIZED SPIRITUALLY AND STRENGTHENED FOR TRIALS. Many times, we think only of singing when we are happy and when times are good, but singing brings strength and energy for our trials. In the book of Acts, Paul and Silas were in prison because of preaching the gospel, so what do they do? They begin to sing!! Many others who have been persecuted for their faith share their stories of how this truth of singing is confirmed. There have been others who have been thrown in prison and have been bound in chains. One pastor shared the story of how they used their chains as musical instruments during their singing. Singing strengthens you and helps you persevere in the face of a trial. Even in our sufferings, we should sing.

Sixth, WHEN YOU SING YOU ENTER THE DOORWAY OF JOY. When you begin to study scripture you will notice that sometimes singing gives birth to joy and sometimes joy gives birth to singing. In scripture, we see that joy and singing are always bound together. If you do a study on joy, you will see singing is involved. If you do a study on singing, you will see joy is involved. It is hard to have one without the other. If you struggle to find joy in your life, then SING! If you are joyful, then SING! In God's perfect design and in His perfect understanding of the human condition He has put joy and singing together for His people. Look at the following scriptures.

"But let all who take refuge in you rejoice;
  let them ever sing for joy,
and spread your protection over them,
  that those who love your name may exult in
you" (Psalms 5:11 ESV).

"I will be glad and exult in you;
  I will sing praise to your name, O Most High"
(Psalms 9:2 ESV).

"Deliver me from bloodguiltiness, O God,
  O God of my salvation,
  and my tongue will sing aloud of
your righteousness" (Psalms 51:14 ESV).

"But I will sing of your strength;
  I will sing aloud of your steadfast love in the
morning.
For you have been to me a fortress
  and a refuge in the day of my distress"
(Psalms 59:16 ESV).

"Because you are my help,
  I sing in the shadow of your wings" (Psalms
63:7 NIV).

Seventh, WHEN YOU SING YOU EXALT AND
GLORIFY GOD. When we obey God, dig deeper
into His Word, build up others, eradicate sin, show
perseverance, and find joy in God, all of these will
exalt God and bring glory to His Holy Name, which
is our purpose in life. We sing to Him and about
Him, this is why we sing. Singing has a unique way
of bringing our hearts, souls, minds, and our
strength together to focus entirely and completely
on God. In an age of where we are distracted so

easily, singing grabs the attention of all our senses and focuses us on God. One day as we gather in Heaven we will all be around the throne of God and what will we be doing? We will be singing His praises. Sing now before God, and sing later before God. If you want victory in your life, then SING!!

CONFESSION TIME

When we come to the end of this stanza we see the psalmist still being oppressed, but in the very last verse, he makes a confession. The psalmist writes, "I have gone astray like a lost sheep." If you go back to verse 5, the psalmist makes this remark, "Oh, that I will be steadfast in keeping Your Word." Taking a look at all of Psalms 119 you realize it is a powerful chapter in the book of Psalms and you notice the "traveling singer", the psalmist is a spiritual man, but yet, he also has a problem staying committed to God. We all struggle at times, and maybe your struggle is to stay committed to God, well, don't despair. Open God's Word and read what it says. Make the Bible the foundation of your life. Allow the Word of God to draw you closer to Christ.

The last part of verse 176 the psalmist states, "I do not forget Your Word." We have probably used the same words, but then as soon as something happens in our life we throw that statement right out the window. We end up with spiritual amnesia. We completely forget to keep His Word. We make promises, the psalmist made promises to not forget God's Word. After reading this whole book and reading the whole 119th chapter, we have seen the psalmist speaking of reading God's Word, meditating on God's Word, and finding delight in God's Word. We have seen that the psalmist was a learner. His secret to not forgetting the Word was to repeatedly expose himself to God's truth so that he would know it, live by it, and never forget it.

SONG FROM THE HEART

I titled the book "The Singing Traveler" for a reason. The psalmist who traveled quite a bit knew how to sing the Word of God. He spent His life being oppressed by those who thought they didn't need the Word, but the psalmist kept doing what verse 172 says. He lifted up his voice and sang praises to God.

"In the year 1742 John Wesley gave these five rules on singing in church:

1. Sing all. See that you join with the congregation as frequently as you can. Let not slight degrees of weakness or weariness hinder you. If it is a cross to you, take it up and you will find a blessing.

2. Sing lustily and with a good courage. Beware of singing as if you were half asleep, but lift up your voice with strength.

3. Sing modestly. Do not bawl so as to be heard above or distinct from the rest of the congregation; but strive to unite your voices together so as to make one clear, melodious sound.

4. Sing in time. Whatever time is sung, be sure to keep with it. Do not run before nor stay behind it.

5. Above all, sing spiritually. Have an eye to God in every word you sing. In order to do this, attend strictly to the sense of what you sing and see that your heart is not carried away with the sound but offered to God continually." [77]

"One summer evening late in the last century a hard-bitten agnostic sat on the banks of the Connecticut River in Massachusetts. Dusk had settled in a blue haze on the mountains across the river. Dimly he glimpsed the lights of the church on a rise just above the village of Northfield. He smiled cynically. Then

drifting across the still water there came the faint sound of a voice singing.

There were ninety and nine that safely lay
In the shelter of the fold,
But one was out on the hills away.
Far off from the gates of gold—
Away on the mountains wild and bare,
Away from the tender Shepherd's care.

The man listened. What a voice it was! The beauty of it fascinated him, but the words—He shrugged off the first two verses, but the third caught him. That voice—its earnestness, it's pleading. As the last note died away the man bent his head and accepted the Shepherd as his Savior and Lord.

On another day, an inveterate criminal slouched against the wall of his cell in a Belfast prison. Suddenly through the barred windows came the sound of music—then a voice singing the well-known "Hold the Fort." Coming from a church at the other end of the block, the voice was faint, but it filled the narrow room. And its tender compassion touched the heart of the hardened criminal. Halfway through the song, he dropped to his knees and before that voice ceased he had believed and was saved. He died a tireless church worker." 78

"A young Christian traveler found himself in a commercial room one night, where, the party being large and merry, it was proposed that each man should sing a song. Many of the usual character on such occasions were sung. It came the turn of our young friend, who excused himself on the ground that he knew no songs they would care to hear. In derision, one present asked him if he could not sing one of Sankey's hymns, and several declared they would join in the chorus. He decided to take them at the word, and with a silent prayer, he chose one of the well-known hymns and sang it as he had perhaps never sung before. All present joined in the chorus. Before its close there were moist eyes and troubled hearts, and several gathered around him thanking him for the song. When he retired, he had not been long in his room when he heard a knock at the door. He opened it to a young traveler who was in deep trouble. The song had brought back to memory the songs his deceased mother had sung. He knew his life was not right, and the inquiry was on his lips, "What must I do to be saved?" He was pointed to Christ. Scarcely had he left when there was another knock; this time, an older man whom the song had reminded of a lost joy and peace. He was a backslider, the singer had the joy of pointing him also to the Savior, and though it was nearly two o'clock before he could lie down, it was with heartfelt gratitude to Him who had honored his personal testimony for Christ." 79

OUR PRAYER

Heavenly Father, we thank You for this psalm and what it teaches us about the Word. Thank You for using the psalmist to write and teach us about life and to show us that even people who seem to be spiritual also struggle with things just like we do. Thank you for the gift of singing, may we always follow Your commands and sing. Thank You most of all for Your Son Jesus. In Jesus Name, Amen.

CONCLUSION

I would encourage you to take Psalms 119 and read it in different translations. I used four different translations for this chapter which gave me a better understanding of what I was reading. When you take the time to study and read this psalm you will find that God's Word is true, pure, good, faithful, right, sweet and wonderful.

When we read and study God's Word we should walk in it, keep, learn, respect, obey, memorize, declare, rejoice, meditate, delight, and remember it. We should understand, choose, and run the way of it. We should observe it, long after it, talk of it, trust, hope, seek, and love it. We should turn to it, give thanks for it, believe it, be sound in it, don't forsake it, consider it and be zealous for it.

When we read and study God's Word, He does things for us. He teaches us, commands us to keep it diligently, illuminates us, and defends us when we obey it. He reveals the Word to us, quickens us, gives us understanding, strengthens us, and graciously grants it to us. He will enlarge our hearts make us go in the path of His commandments. He will bring it to our remembrance, comfort us with it, and save us because we seek it. With His Word, we become wiser than our enemies, He upholds us with it, and He orders our steps and delivers us. When we stray He will seek us because we remember His Words.

"Let me tell you about some dear friends of mine: "Punk" and "Beanie" Peters. Punk's real name was Ralph; Beanie's was Lavena. They were members of Driftwood Christian Church near Vallonia, Indiana. Beanie was a simple farm wife who had an unshakable faith.

Dying of liver cancer, I was at the hospital with her family, essentially on a deathwatch. Beanie's pain was excruciating, and the pain medicine kept her in a nearly unconscious state. Others left the room for a moment; only her daughter Harriet and Punk were present with me. Suddenly Beanie opened her eyes.

Looking at the ceiling, she said, "Sing." I leaned over her bed and asked, "What did you say Beanie?"

"Sing."

"Do you want us to sing a hymn?"

She nodded. So I started:

*"I heard an old, old story, how a Savior who came
from glory..." By that time Ralph and Harriet joined in:
"How He gave His life on Calvary to save a wretch
like me;
I heard about His groaning, and His precious blood
atoning;
Then I repented of my sin and won the victory."*

*On the chorus, Beanie joined us. She sang the
melody; Harriet sang alto; Punk sang tenor, and I
picked up the bass.*

*"Oh, victory in Jesus! My Savior forever;
He sought me and bought me
With His redeeming blood
He loved me 'ere I knew Him
And all my love is due Him
He plunged me to victory beneath the cleansing
flood."*

*I started singing the last verse. With eyes fastened on
the ceiling, Beanie's voice became stronger:*

*"I heard about a mansion He has built for me in Glory
And I heard about the streets of gold beyond the
crystal sea;
About the angels' singing the old redemption story;
And some sweet day I'll sing up there the song of
victory!"*

Sing the chorus with me.

"Victory in Jesus, my Savior forever!"

We prayed together, and hours later, Beanie Peters died. Just a few years later her daughter Harriet died of the same type of cancer. Not long ago, Punk also went home to be with the Lord. Out of the four in that room, I am the only one left to tell the story. No matter what trials you face, sing. God is there to help you through." 80

There are some major themes that I noticed as I was reading and studying while writing this book.

First we need to continually sing as we travel. We should always carry a song in our heart as we read, study and memorize the Word of God. We need to be as the psalmist and sing as we travel, lift up our voices in praise seven times a day.

Second the Word of God should become sweet to us; we should become addicted to the Word, just like we are addicted to chocolate, food, exercise, or whatever our addiction might be. Keep reading the Word and tasting how sweet it really is.

Third we should be broken over the ones that despise the Word of God. We should not complain about them, but we should cry over them and over their lack of interest in following what God says in the Bible.

Fourth we need to sing, sing, and sing. Pentatonix, the acapella group that is so popular has a song called, "Sing." My daughter bought the CD for me for Christmas. I want to leave with you with some of the lyrics.

"It doesn't matter if your days are long (Sing!)
It doesn't matter if your night's gone wrong (Sing!)
Just clap your hands and stomp your feet and sing it
(Whoa, sing!)
It doesn't matter if you're way off track (Sing!)
Feel like you're headed for a heart attack (Sing!)
Just raise your voice and bring the noise and sing it
(Whoa, sing!)

Sing, sing, sing, sing
Sing it out as hard as you can
Make 'em hear ya from LA to Japan
Don't let 'em bring you down
This is how we do it now
Go and roll them windows down and
Sing, sing, sing, sing
Sing it with your hands in the sky

Light it up like it's the 4th of July
Don't let 'em bring you down
You know what I'm talking 'bout
A little bit louder now" 81

SOURCES

1. www.beautifulquotes/quotes/author/l/Lailah_gif ty_akita.html

2. www.inspirationalquotes4u.com/singing/index.ht ml Maya Angelou

3. www.goodreads.com/quotes/tag/hebrew-alphabet/ Michael Ben Zehabe, *The Meaning of Hebrew Letters: A Hebrew Language Program for Christians*

4. www.searchquotes.com/search/Dont_Leave_Me /Author unknown

5. www.sermoncentral.com/illustrations/sermon-illustration-rich-young-quotes-obedience-faith-doinggodswill

6. www.thinkexist.com/quotes/willie_sutton

7. www.sermoncentral.com/sermons/the-value-of-gods-word-stephen-elmer-sermon-on-bible-influence

8. www.personal.umich.edu/~pfa/poemquot/open. html/clara h scott

9. www.dreamthisday.com/quotes-sayings/faithfulness/mother_teresa

10. www.godwithus-org-au.com/Reverend_rogelio_bucao

11. "The Patriot": Perseverance despite Heartbreak, Citation: The Patriot, rated R, Columbia Pictures, Centropolis Entertainment; Executive Producers,

William Fay, Ute Emmerich, Roland Emmerich; submitted by David Slagle, Lawrenceville, Georgia]

12. www.thinkexist.com/quotations/repentance/thomas j watson
13. www.gracechurch.org/sfellowship/pulpitcm/article. "Praying For the Right Things/john_macarthur
14. www.goodreads.com/quotes/tag/bible/ronald_reagan
15. www.christianpost.com/news/greg-laurie-is-it-acceptable-for-christians-to-drink-86161/
16. www.searchquotes.com/search/Keep_Singing/
17. www.songlyrics.com/kathy-troccoli/a-different-road-lyrics/
18. www.freebiblestudyguides.org/bible-teachings/armor-of-god.jpg
19. www.sermonillustrations.com/a-z/s/spiritual_warfare.htm/Craig Brian Larson
20. www.goodreads.com/author/quotes/William_Booth
21. www.searchquotes.com/quotes/author/Giuseppe_Garibaldi/
22. www.mastersvoice.com/album/new-grace
23. www.salvationarmyusa.org/usn/red-kettle-history
24. www.christianitytoday.com/ch/131christians/activists/williambooth.html
25. www.searchquotes.com/search/Things_Will_Work_Out/
26. www.focusongod.com/broken1.htm

27. www.sermonsearch.com/sermon-illustrations/6344/a-song-in-the-heart/

28. www.searchquotes.com/quotes/author/Vivian_Greene/

29. www.foxnews.com/entertainment/2013/06/19/which-celebrity-is-worst-role-model-for-kids/

30. Noah E. McCormick/sermon/ Serve/Love/Live Eastside Baptist Church, Collinsville, OK

31. www.mtstandard.com/sports/good-bad-role-models/article.html

32. www.sermonsearch.com/sermon-illustrations/4098/model/

33. www.brainyquote.com/quotes/quotes/r/robertfrant_despair/robert frank

34. G. Campbell Morgan /The Westminster Pulpit, vol. ix, pp. 318-323.

35. www.harvest.org/devotions-and-blogs/daily-devotions/corrie_ten_boom

36. bibleornot.org/its-it-is-always-darkest-before-the-dawn/

37. www.christianity.com/church/church-history/church-history-for-kids/j-s-bach-soli-deo-gloria-to-the-glory-of-god-alone.html

38. www.thoughts-about-god.com/quotes/quotes-god.htm

39. www.songlyrics.com/casting-crowns/the-word-is-alive-lyrics/

40. www.songlyrics.com/casting-crowns/the-word-is-alive-lyrics/

41. www.sermoncentral.com/sermons/the-word-of-god--it8217s-alive-j-jeffrey-smead-sermon-on-bible-truth

42. www.sermoncentral.com/sermons/the-word-of-god--it8217s-alive-j-jeffrey-smead-sermon-on-bible-truth

43. getmorestrength.org/daily/sweeter-than-honey/joe_stowell

44. Sweeter than Chocolate, Developing a Healthy Addiction to God's Word, 2014, Christy Bower

45. Sweeter than Chocolate, Developing a Healthy Addiction to God's Word, 2014, Christy Bower

46. www.hotsermons.com/sermon-illustrations/sermon-illustrations-gods-word.html

47. www.quotegarden.com/light.html/michael_strassfeld

48. www.sermoncentral.com/sermons/gods-word-lights-our-way-dennis-davidson-sermon-on-gods-word-182829.asp?Page=5

49. Sweeter than Chocolate, Developing a Healthy Addiction to God's Word, 2014, Christy Bower

50. www.science.nationalgeographic.com/science/space/universe/power-of-light/

51. www.thinkexist.com/quotes/shinichi_suzuki/

52. www.sermonillustrations.com/a-z/p/peer_pressure.htm Charles Swindoll, Living Above the Level of Mediocrity

53. www.sermoncentral.com/illustrations/sermon-illustration-pastor-brad-henry-stories-fearandworry-80523.asp

54. www.youtube.com/watch?v=h97kbv4mbsc

55. www.sermoncentral.com/sermons/time-for-god-to-act-tim-byrd-sermon-on-bible-influence

56. www.moreillustrations.com/Illustrations/sowing_reaping.html

57. www.sermoncentral.com/illustrations/sermon-illustration-sermon-central-staff-quotes-bibleinfluence-79894.asp, R.G. Lee

58. www.quotes.inspirational.com/quotes/tears/billy_graham

59. www.debate.org/opinions/is-the-bible-really-the-word-of-god

60. www.debate.org/opinions/is-the-bible-really-the-word-of-god.

61. www.goodreads.com/quotes/34690-people-don-t-care-how-much-you-know-until-they-know

62. www.acdlaonline.com/zoomdocs/presentations/Billy_Moore_bio.pdf

63. www.leadershipnow.com/passionquotes.html/henri_amiel

64. www.beliefnet.com/Quotes/Christian/A/A-W-Tozer/The-Bible-Is-Not-An-End-In-Itself-But-A-Means-To.aspx

65. www.hotsermons.com/sermon-illustrations/sermon-illustrations-gods-word.html

66. www.hotsermons.com/sermon-illustrations/sermon-illustrations-gods-word.html

67. www.searchquotes.com/search/Sleepless/2/

68. www.statisticbrain.com/sleeping-disorder-statistics/

69. www.pen-of-the-wayfarer.blogspot.com/2009/01/spurgeon-on-psalm-32.html

70. "The Old Man and the Gulls" from Paul Harvey's The Rest of the Story by Paul Aurandt, 1977, quoted in Heaven Bound Living, Knofel Stanton, Standard, 1989, pp. 79-80.

71. www.tentmaker.org/Quotes/truthquotes.htm

72. www.sermoncentral.com/illustrations/sermon-illustration-paddick-van-zyl-stories-court-bloodofjesus-christredeems

73. www.quotes-inspirational.com/quote/life-inner-peace-being-harmonious

74. www.people.com/people/archive/article.html/tracy_lippard

75. www.sermoncentral.com/sermons/cease-fire-finding-a-peace-that-lasts-melvin-newland-sermon-on-peace

76. www.quotes-inspirational.com/quotes/singing/ella_fitzgerald

77. www.moreillustrations.com/Illustrations/singing.html

78. www.moreillustrations.com/Illustrations/singing.html

79. www.moreillustrations.com/Illustrations/singing.html

80. www.sermoncentral.com/illustrations/sermon-illustration-thomas-cash-stories-peace

81. www.lyrics.com/sing-lyrics-pentatonix.html

www.ingramcontent.com/pod-product-compliance
Lightning Source LLC
Chambersburg PA
CBHW051812090426
42736CB00011B/1435